BEAUTY SECRETS

BEAUTY SECRETS
Women
and the
Politics of
Appearance

Wendy Chapkis

Photos: Gon Buurman

SOUTH END PRESS

Production by South End Press, USA
Manufactured in the USA
Cover photo by Francesca Sullivan, cover design by Lydia Sargent
Photographs by Gon Buurman, unless otherwise specified

Library of Congress Cataloging-in-Publication Data

Chapkis, W. (Wendy)
   Beauty secrets.
   Bibliography: p. 205
   Includes index.
   1. Feminine beauty (Aesthetics)   2. Femininity
(Psychology)   3. Sex role.   I. Title.
HQ1219.C47   1986   646.7'042   86-21916
ISBN 0-89608-280-6
ISBN 0-89608-279-2 (pbk.)

® GCIU   745-C

For Margie, Bob, Steve, and Karen

———

Table of Contents

Secrets

Two American children on a family holiday in Europe believe English to be a private language. The children are seeing the sights, including me: "It's a man, check out the moustache," he says. "It's a woman. Look at the earrings," she says. "It's a man. That's a moustache!" "Okay, it is a moustache, but look at the clothes." I want to stop them, to fade away, to respond. But I can't manage anything at all. I feel frozen and sick. And totally exposed.

Strolling through a small Greek town, I am greeted with shouts of "Hey Moustache!" "Yeah, what?" I yell back. That isn't the reply I want to make. Still, it's *something*. I have to fight my inclination to silently slink away. That evening at dinner, I nervously scan a group of young men at the next table—much as I might once have done in anticipation of sexual advances but now in fear of ridicule. Their table is so crowded that a newcomer turns to me to ask if the extra chair is free. Relieved this is all he intends, I smile broadly and offer it to him. He stops, looks more closely and roars, "Hey look at this—a moustache! I thought you were a man, but you're a woman! Ha!" Still trying for the appropriate comeback, I answer "Yes, I see you've got one too." "But *I*," he actually thumps his chest, "am a *man*."

In the tram in Amsterdam, I sit engrossed in a book, on my way to a party. I am dressed up and have even, a few hours earlier, plucked most of the hairs from my chin. I feel beautiful and anonymous. I can pass, fit in, quietly read my book. But gradually I become aware of the three men behind me not just being obnoxiously loud in general, they are hooting with laughter about *me*. I glance up as the one closest puts out his hand and rubs my chin: "Is it possible? This is a woman? Look guys—with a moustache and a beard!" I feel cold all over; my festive mood and attire suddenly ridiculously out of place. "Go to hell" and I pretend to return to my book. So self-conscious have I become that I even remember to turn the pages at appropriate intervals. And I hold

1

back my tears. For days afterwards, I re-live the scene and fantasize more empowering endings.

And then I surrender. I make my first appointment with Dorothy. Dorothy is perhaps fifty and motherly in a professional sort of way. She is a "beauty specialist," an expert in making women like me beautiful. Or at least acceptable.

Dorothy spends fifteen minutes burning hairs out of my chin with jolts of electricity. My chin. I am still filled with shame. I am a feminist. How humiliated I then feel. I am a woman. How ugly I have been made to feel. I have failed on both counts. For years, I've displayed my hairy underarms and legs with defiant pride. But the hairy face is unusual and hence "unnatural" for a woman. And ugly. God help me, I too think it ugly. I too look askance at older women with their bristly chins. They disturb me; the hairy faces match their crumpled clothing and seemingly unconnected lives. Their faces too often speak of defeat not pride in challenging convention.

The rest of us, whose smoothly anonymous faces hide our secrets, look quickly away. We are reminded of what will happen if we are not ever vigilant. I am left without support, no role models. Left with despairing faces and their hairy chins.

Not since the height of pubescent self-consciousness have I felt such concern about my appearance. Never before have I felt such fear of ridicule. In every other way, I "fit"—I am white, slim and tall. Those areas where I differed from the norm were always chosen. They represented acts of self-conscious rebellion.

I evolved from a "cute" southern California blond in the 1960s to a radical San Francisco Bay Area feminist in the early 1970s. That radical feminist naturally rejected the very California Girl standard of beauty I had once cultivated. I adopted the somewhat sullen, but politically correct, blue jeans, no make-up and hair wherever it grew Look.

When I moved out of that supportive feminist ghetto, I found to my shock that I had become "ugly." And I had no idea how to respond.

Rather than righteous anger, I knew only shame. As a feminist I felt I had "no business" feeling stung by not measuring up. Of course I *knew* that all my sisters felt comfortable in their skins—whatever shape, color, texture, or size they happened to be.

It was that "less feminist than thou" guilt that prevented me from turning to other women with my confusions. I kept my problem a private if burning secret. And when I no longer felt able to resist, I chose the most private of solutions, electrolysis. After each "treatment," I hid my swollen face; keeping my answer as utterly secret as my problem.

But it didn't matter. Because a few weeks after the swelling went down, a few weeks after the scabs disappeared, the hairs began to grow back. "Well, it's like that," I am told. "Sometimes it takes years to totally destroy all the hair follicles."

I pass yet another young man on the street who feels obliged to offer his judgement of me. He stops in my path and stares. "Hey moustache." And without thinking, I reach out, grab his bare arm and dig my fingernails in deep. I walk on carrying chunks of flesh away with me. It has its effect; surprise and fear replace his mocking grin. He looks back at me like I'm crazy. Dangerous crazy.

Is this, then, the empowering conclusion I have been fantasizing? Maybe not but it feels good. It feels very good. Only it doesn't last any longer than the electrolysis.

Apparently each isolated act of violence, like personal abuse, is too private to be a real solution. But going beyond private solutions means breaking the silence. And I still don't think my problem should matter. It shouldn't matter enough to tell. It shouldn't matter so much that I could be so afraid to tell.

And yet I know that there can be no truly empowering conclusions until our beauty secrets are shared.

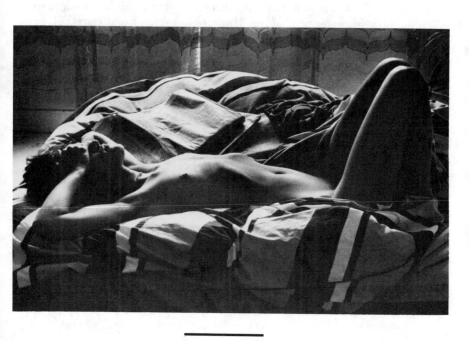

1
Changing
Landscapes

"Mommy, why do you have a moustache?" asks the child in the Removatron Hair Removal ad. "Because sometimes even nature makes mistakes...unwanted facial hair can be embarrassing...put an end to those embarrassing questions...you'll be glad you did."

The moustached woman—like all women who fail to conform—is not only Other she is Error; flawed both in her failure to be a normal male and in her inability to appear as a normal female. Though this judgement is intrinsically impersonal, it is rarely experienced that way. Each woman is somehow made to feel an intensely private shame for her "personal failure." She is alone in the crowd pushing toward the cosmetics counter, the plastic surgeon, the beauty specialist. "Epilator 2700" reminds those in the industry how lucrative this belief can be:

> Hair removal is no doubt one of the fastest growing profit specialities in the beauty world today. It is estimated that 85% to 90% of all women have unwanted facial or body hair. Many of these people go to great lengths to solve this often embarrassing beauty problem.

We are like foreigners attempting to assimilate into a hostile culture, our bodies continually threatening to betray our difference. Each of us who seeks the rights of citizenship through acceptable femininity shares a secret with all who attempt to pass: my undisguised self is unacceptable, I am not what I seem. To successfully pass is to be momentarily wrapped in the protective cover of conformity. To fail is to experience the vulnerability of the outsider.

Despite the fact that each woman knows her own belabored transformation from female to feminine is artificial, she harbors the secret conviction that it should be effortless. A "real woman" would be naturally feminine while she is only in disguise. To the uninitiated—men—the image must maintain its mystery, hence the tools of

5

transformation are to be hidden away as carefully as the "flaws" they are used to remedy.

Consider the difference between the public display of the masculine straight razor and shaving soap and the carefully concealed tweezer or depilatory secreted away in a woman's cosmetics case. For the removal of body hair, there is no female counterpart to the reassuring image of father, face lathered and razor in hand, daily reminding his family and himself of his manhood in the morning ritual of shaving. Advertisements make almost heroic the act of a manly He shaving away thick stubble while an admiring She looks lustfully on. Imagine a similar cultural celebration of a woman plucking her eyebrows, shaving her armpits or waxing her upper lip. All advertisements for products to de-hair the female show only the aftereffects; "before" scenes apparently would be too shocking.

Even more public acts of femininity, like applying make-up, tend to rely on an underlying message of female inadequacy. There is a problem to be corrected, a basic improvement to be made:

> Problems: My eyes look pale and washed out. My nose is too wide at the bottom. Can you show me what to do so my lips don't look so thin? How can I soften the line of my pointy chin?
> Solution: Merel Norman personalized skin care and make-up.

Women begin early in life with this sense that we aren't quite right. During childhood the identification of woman as other and less lays the groundwork for all forms of inequality. But appearance is the first, constant commentary. As a woman comes to accept her physical "difference" as evidence of personal failure, she also learns to share society's belief that hostility is her due. This experience of inadequacy means that no woman is allowed to say or to believe "I am beautiful."

In a women's writing workshop, we are given the following assignment: "Look at the woman on your left. Study her for a moment and then jot down one word that comes to mind as you look at her. Give her the paper. Now each of us will write for three minutes about that word."

My word is "golden"; my neighbor's is "apple." The interesting thing about the drill is not how well each of us can write, the choice of metaphors and nice turns of phrase. It is the content that is gripping. Not one of the descriptive words passed along is remotely critical. We are all careful of the responsibility not to wound each other by offering up words like "fat," "stringy," or even "glasses" or "gray." We all pass on words of power, pleasure or beauty. But what we have done with those words...

"Golden," I write, "goldy locks, gold plated, the Midas Touch, all that glitters is not..." My neighbor takes "apple" and writes "shiney and pretty to look at but watch out for the worms. Sleeping Beauty and the poison apple..." Not one of us could take the word and proclaim, "I am good. I am deserving of this praise."

The rise of the second wave of feminism in the United States was heralded by demonstrations at the Miss America pageant in 1968. A Freedom Trash Can was provided by picketers into which women could throw bras, girdles, wigs, curlers. This challenge to commercial codes of beauty and privatized shame earned feminists the media tag "Bra Burners."

A few years later, my eight year old sister wrote a school essay about me: "Wendy is a feminist. When I grow up, I am going to be just like her except I'll dress better." Now, more than a decade gone by, I think her prophetic—only these days I dress better too. Despite my updated wardrobe (my flannels and jeans now share closet space with leather pants, a dress or two and flourescent pink T-shirts), I am no less concerned about the politics of appearance. Today my twenty year old sister looks uncomfortably down at our hairy legs: "I don't have any problems with equal rights, sexual preference or fighting racism in the movement. But, hey Wendy, why is it we still can't shave?"

Ten or fifteen years ago we weren't allowed to display body hair and believe ourselves to be acceptable and sexual. And apparently we still aren't. A long decade after resolutions were passed against the sexual objectification of women's bodies and in favor of abolishing artifical gender distinctions, we are turning again to one another with doubts and confusions.

We know we fail as women to be "feminine enough" (by choice we reassuringly remind one another) and we fear we fail as feminists because we are still concerned about whether we are "attractive" (let alone to whom). Even more disturbing, we are beginning to suspect that while a genderless sisterhood may have made for wholesome family relations, it may not be the stuff of erotic fantasy.

Much of our joy in doing battle with sexism has been replaced with grim determination. Perhaps this is the inevitable result of ten years in which we changed faster than the world around us. In the early days of the movement, the call to resist gender stereotyping in appearance promised empowerment: we would create our own images of womanhood not measured against the feminine ideal. Those heady days of militant rejection have stretched into the long haul. The standards by which we are judged and self-critically judge ourselves remain much the same.

Though feminism has changed the way women view the world and themselves, it often feels as if the world has turned feminism into a new kind of lip gloss. The daring insistence of early feminists that a woman is beautiful just as she naturally appears has been rewritten in a commercial translation as the Natural Look. The horrible irony of this is, of course, that only a handful of women have the Natural Look naturally. Most of us have flaws that must be disguised if we are to resemble the beautiful models setting the standard—a fact the beauty industry is banking on.

No question that it was liberating to free hips from the binding of the girdle, breasts from the confines of a push-up bra, faces from the mask of heavy make-up. But the current ideal beauty remains a narrow-hipped, high-breasted woman with flawless skin. While the standards show little more flexibility and variety than in the past, women are now supposed to attain them without visible artifice.

This insistence on natural beauty has created two new categories of "attractive" women: the child-woman made popular by American film star Brooke Shields, and the over forty physically fit midlife beauty (Jane Fonda, Raquel Welch and company). These women, though a generation apart, embody a cultural fantasy of unaffected (free from artifice) and unchanging (forever young) beauty.

A girl at the edge of puberty has a naturally hairless body that demands no shaving, waxing or chemicals to feel smooth. She has the soft, wrinkle-free skin of childhood older women can only regain with surgery and careful application of creams and cosmetics. Skin her slightly older acne stricken sisters struggle to recapture with make-up and astringents. Her body is naturally small, supple and nothing if not youthful.

The over-forty beauty shares with the child-woman the promise of eternal youth. To be beautiful, they seem to say, is to look a constant twenty whether biologically twelve or forty-five. Now that foundation garments and heavy make-up (which provided the illusion of youth) have fallen out of fashion, older women must literally remake

their bodies in the pursuit of beauty. Scientific skin care, cosmetic surgery vand fitness programs promise to minimize the visible changes of living.

Thus, despite the fact that the "baby boom" generation is reaching midlife, beauty remains adolescent. Even with the growing visibility of older women, their most striking quality is their apparent youth.

As columnist Ellen Goodman notes, these women do not so much challenge our ideas about beauty as they:

> raise the threshold of self-hate faster than the age span...those of us who failed to look like Brooke Shields at seventeen can now fail to look like Victoria Principal at thirty-three and like Linda Evans at forty-one and like Sophia Loren at fifty. When Gloria Steinem turned fifty this year she updated her famous line from forty. She said, "This is what fifty looks like." With due apologies to the cult of midlife beauty, allow me two words: "Not necessarily."[1]

The midlife beauties would most likely agree. It apparently takes hard work and concerted effort to maintain beauty over forty; several of these women are making a fortune on the sales of books outlining exactly that position. Clearly the appeal of Jane Fonda's *Workout*, Linda Evans' *Beauty and Exercise Book* and Raquel Welch's *Total Beauty and Fitness Program* lies in the promise that they can get you in shape— *their* shape. The over-forty beauties' insistence on energetic exercise seems to suggest that the older body, left to itself, is lazy, undisciplined and out of control. "Skin repair" advertisements echo this message:

> ...over time your skin gets lazier and lazier. And it doesn't produce new cells as fast or as frequently as it once did...Buf Puf Gentle promotes the rebirth of your skin...Age-control-ling cream by Estee Lauder...encourages all skin to do what young skin does on its own.

The woman who "lets herself go" and shows her age clearly only has herself and her lack of discipline to blame:

> The ugly truth is we all age...No need to panic...La Prairie Cellular Skincare Preparations...ease the visible signs of age-ing. The over forty look is over...you can actually feel your dull, tired-looking skin respond to Radiant Action. The fact is, from this moment on beautiful skin is simply a matter of Discipline...rewarding you with skin that is sleek...Skin that has been disciplined. There are no miracles. There is only Discipline.

The acknowledged queen of physically fit midlife beauty, Jane Fonda, is a remarkably disciplined woman. She is an accomplished actress, film producer, political activist, businesswoman, mother, partner and fitness fanatic. She is also a woman with a history of twenty-three years of bulimia—of compulsive eating and induced vomiting. With characteristic courage, Fonda went public with her painful history:

> Society says we have to be thin, and while most of us don't have much control over our lives, we can control our weight, either by starving to death or by eating all we want and not showing the effects...I loved to eat, but I wanted to be wonderfully thin. It didn't take long for me to become a serious bulimic—binging and purging fifteen to twenty times a day! ...bulimia was my secret "vice." No one was supposed to find out about it, and because I was supposed to be so strong and perfect, I couldn't admit to myself that I had weaknesses and a serious disease.[2]

In her attempt to maintain a perpetually thin and youthful beauty, Fonda was faced with the choice of starving to death (stay pretty, die young) or control (not showing the effects of eating, of aging). If bulimia was Jane Fonda's secret vice, fitness is her public virtue. And yet the objective of both is remarkably similar—live but don't change. Maintain an attractive appearance through the disciplined exercise of control over the body.

This is not to say that there is nothing to choose between working out and throwing up. Obviously fitness—unlike bulimia—has positive and particular value for women. Physical strength can undoubtedly increase a woman's sense of personal power, just as building muscular "definition" can be a means of literally attaining a more distinct sense of self. This is especially true for those people—older women very much included—who have experienced a lack of social and physical identity. Stephen Greco suggests a similar appeal among gay men for body building:

> With bulk and definition, gay amateur body-building can compensate for the powerlessness and invisibility some say are ours as "marginal" members of society...the point is not merely the clarity of muscle groups under the skin, or a child's idea of the look of powerfulness, but the existential clarity that comes from the individual articulating for himself his presence in the world. That's power.[3]

But is it? Taking control of the kind of body image to be presented to the world *can* be empowering—though it then seems a bit feeble to choose the shape that is currently most fashionable. Perhaps more to the point is the exhilerating experience of pushing past previous limits. This can build confidence that might enable a woman to do the same in a social or political context. It can, but it doesn't necessarily work that way.

After all, fitness training is an intensely individual process. You are your only obstacle at the weight machine and no one else can help push those pounds. But the workout metaphor is a less useful guide to attaining power in the workplace, home or community where collective effort is essential. Fitness imagery does speak, though, to a world in recession. Bite the bullet and go for the burn.

It, in fact, may well be the recession climate that makes so attractive the idea of getting in shape: the exercise of control over the body compensating for a basic sense of a life out of control; a body that says "that's power" substituting for real authority. If this is the case, fitness may not represent a revolution in female beauty standards as much as it does the latest in beauty fashion. One that reflects increased expectations and equally high insecurity among women. And it echoes the very old promise that beauty is the answer to both.

Fitness promises not only a better shot at outrunning the competition but also offers the possibility of winning the race on points. A physically fit female body will attract the favorable attention of the judges. *Vogue UK* recently assured its readers:

> The fitness commitment may be unisex, but it is not asexual. Whereas the sixties taught that sex was healthy, the eighties hold that health is sexy...Mariel Hemingway crouching to touch her Nikes on the starting line is every bit as feminine as Jean Harlow bending to paint her toenails in the boudoir..."[4]

Apparently not to Hemingway herself, however, who followed her screen appearance as a muscular athlete with a real-life breast enlargement operation because she reportedly had never felt adequately feminine in her old body.[5]

Those who would dispute the idea that the ultimate appeal of female fitness is the promise of timeless beauty and not strength or health should reflect on the fact that the models of the muscular look tend to be film stars not athletes. In an article on "Real Life Fitness," *U.S. Vogue* remarks: "When we think of good body today we don't think Marilyn Monroe; we think of Jane Fonda; we think of Jessica Lange..."[6]

But do we think of Billy Jean King who at fifteen was told by a tennis coach that she would be good "not because of her ability but because she was ugly?"[7]

Or of Jarmila Kratochvilova, the champion runner from Czechoslovakia who was subject to constant mockery in the Western press for failing to look feminine enough: "Her achievements...at the World Athletic Championships...have been belittled even as they were being recorded...how shocking, her chest is flat and muscular...She is not acceptably pretty and—good gracious—her legs are 'muscular and hairy.' "[8]

Or of Carolyn Cheshire, the top female body-builder in the UK about whom it has been observed: "It is, of course, fortunate for her that she has delicate features and a graceful demeanour."[9]

While female muscles may be in, pretty clearly only certain kinds of muscles on certain kinds of recognizably feminine bodies are really acceptable. The model of the youthful and physically fit woman ultimately is not a symbol of power so much as it is a symbol of the beauty of feminine control over appetites and age.

Among women, feeling fat, like feeling out of shape, has long been a metaphor for feeling powerless. Dieting and fitness training can be seen as attempts to regain control. In a 1984 body image survey done by *Glamour Magazine*[10] of 33,000 women, more than three-quarters reported feeling too fat while according to height/weight tables only one quarter could be so described. Part of this negative body distortion can be attributed to comparisons each woman makes between her body and the currently fashionable underweight media model. Even Jane Fonda goes on a crash diet when preparing to shoot a film because she believes that the cameras "make her appear fifteen pounds overweight."[11] But the problem goes deeper.

In the *Glamour Magazine* study, psychologist Dr. Wooley notes, "Dieting is often a self-cure for depression and other ills. It gives women a sense of control, of doing something about problems—families, jobs, sex—that may have nothing to do with their bodies." Dr. Hilde Bruch, authority on *anorexia nervosa* (a disease of self-starvation primarily affecting young women) describes anorexics as having a deficient sense of identity and suffering from "an all-pervasive conviction of being ineffective, of having no control over their own lives..." Their response is to exercise punishing control over the body. "Many experience themselves and their bodies as separate entities, and it is the mind's task to control the unruly and despised body."[12]

While the anorexic may first simply appear to be pursuing the contemporary ideal of slender beauty, her body soon becomes a grim parody of "thin and trim." In her extreme, the anorexic sheds light on a far more universal conflict between female body, beauty and autonomy. Until that conflict is resolved, each attempt to redefine female beauty will result in little more than a change of fashion.

However much the particulars of the beauty package may change from decade to decade—curves in or out, skin delicate or ruddy, figures fragile or fit—the basic principles remain. The body beautiful is woman's responsibility and authority. She will be valued and rewarded on the basis of how close she comes to embodying the ideal. Whatever the current borders of beauty, they will always be well-defined and exceedingly narrow, and it will be woman's task to conform to them—for as long as is humanly possible. While beauty is a "timeless" quality, the beautiful woman is tightly fettered to time. Female beauty is a state to be attained *and lost*.

These constant features of beauty are deeply rooted in Western culture. In the Platonic tradition, beauty is understood as a singular, uniform, unchanging and eternal form; something beyond the physical body. Beauty, says Plato, is "an everlasting loveliness which neither comes nor goes, which neither flowers nor fades, for such beauty is the same on every hand, the same then as now, here as there, this way as that way, the same to every worshipper as it is to every other."[13] Beauty is thus removed from the diverse and changing world of the living, for while Platonic beauty may be everlasting and uniform, bodies are neither.

The relationship between Beauty and body is thus extremely problematic, all the more so for women for whom both qualities are central to identity. Approximating beauty can be essential to a woman's chances for power, respect and attention. Recognizing this, women have quite sensibly directed great energy toward evaluating and improving their appearance. Plato, among others, scornfully notes this typically female preoccupation; fools that they are, women don't seem to realize that the female body can never be Beauty. Beauty, Plato reminds us, cannot "take the form of the face, or of hands, or of anything that is of the flesh."[14]

Never mind that it has always been men who have organized the beauty pageant, serving as presenter, judge and prize-giver; nor that it has been men who have determined that female beauty is very much a question of the flesh. Still, while men, like women, may mistake a pleasing body for Beauty, it is but a momentary confusion. As soon as the beautiful female begins to show evidence of age, mortality, change, the distinction between body and Beauty is restored.

To be alive is to experience an inevitable and uncontrollable process of physical change. The body grows, ages and dies regardless of human will and intervention. In our culture, so unable to accept death, it is not surprising that beauty should be perceived as remote from the changes of life.

Standing at the sink, I disinterestedly watch myself prepare to perform the three-times-daily ritual of cleaning my teeth. Just before the toothbrush reaches my mouth, I stop, staring at my arm. Loose folds of skin nestle in the bend of my right elbow. I muster a short laugh and resolutely carry on with the business at hand. But I am frightened by this new evidence of age. Can this be *my* body starting to sag? Obviously I still don't believe in my own mortality. This realization is as disturbing as the folds of flesh—I know that until I can accept that *this* body will itself be old, until I come to see *myself* in the older bodies around me, all my hearty pronouncements on the beauty of age ring hollow. Viewing the elderly as an oppressed minority is a trick of cowardice: we are all the old; for some of us it just doesn't yet show.

Women and men both learn fear of and distain for the mortal body and seek to escape its limits. Men, asserting independence from the body, identify themselves as soul or mind. The physical is then projected onto women. In a fascinating article on the "somatophobia" inherent in the philosophy of Plato, Elizabeth Spellman notes the

> ...mixture of fear, awe, and disgust in men's attitudes toward the physical world, the body, the woman. Men have purchased one-way tickets to Transcendence in their attempt to deny, or conquer and control, the raging Immanence they see in themselves and project onto women.[15]

While men are busy conquering and controlling nature and woman, women are obsessed with controlling their own bodies. Man believes he survives through his enduring achievements. Woman is her mortal body. A man's relationship to his body, then, appears to be less fraught with tension than a woman's. The male mind can afford to be a much more lenient master over the body, indulging in the appetites of the flesh. A man may sweat, scar and age; none of these indications of physicality and mortality are seen to define the male self. Indeed, those men who take an unseemly interest in the body are described as womanly and presumed to be homosexual. For a man to recognize the male body as Beauty is to be forced to recognize physical change and mortality; in effect condemning himself and his fellows to death.

Concern over control of the flesh (dieting, sexual self-control, disciplining the body against the signs of age) is a particularly feminine obsession. Though woman is identified with body she never can be confidently convinced she is mistress over it. Graying, wrinkling, gaining weight, all represent reminders that the one area of female identity and authority is only marginally governable. The body continually becomes Other until it finally ceases to exist at all; a particularly disturbing proposition for those reduced to no more than their bodies.

For a woman, then, her traditional—if entirely unreliable—ticket to success in life and transcendence beyond it is the mortal body. The woman who is awarded the title of Beauty momentarily escapes into the eternal ideal. Yet she knows, as each woman must, that she has been or will be seen as ugly in her lifetime. To be beautiful is to exist in a moment framed by expectation and fear. We thus deny ourselves pleasures in the special challenges and changing appearances of childhood, youth, maturity and old age in pursuit of a picture perfect moment.

The photographic metaphor is apt. The world of beautiful images photographed for fashion spreads and for the movie and TV screen is not only impossibly perfect but entirely static. One of the appeals of such programs as the internationally popular "Dynasty" is its continual perfect moment. The life of the Carrington's represents the ultimate expression of Beauty and Success as a state to be attained. And these people unquestionably have *arrived*. Even the sanitized tragedies that befall them are meant as proof that Real Beauty and True Success endure. Problems which would disfigure, defeat or destroy lesser creatures leave the stars fundamentally unaltered. So too is age used as evidence of success, not as a threat to it. The midlife trio of Linda Evans, Joan Collins and Diane Carroll (all over forty) prove week after week that Real Beauty defies the changes of time.

In reality, though, the female body is a constantly changing landscape. From the budding breasts of adolescence, through the rounded belly of pregnancy and generous curves of maturity, to the smooth chest of mastectomy and deep creases of old age, our bodies weather and reshape. To call beauty only the still life of unchanging "perfection" is no praise for creatures so lively and diverse as womankind.

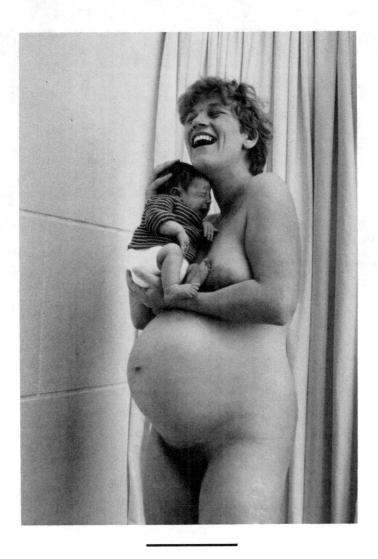

Ann

Photo: Deborah Hoffmann

Ann

"What I look like really looks so different"

At eleven or twelve, I became aware that I was different. I was really pissed off because the other girls started wearing stockings and garter belts—and I couldn't because with diastrophic dwarfism, my legs were too short. I was very aware that this was crucial to growing up, to womanhood.

I asked my sister point-blank "how different do I look?" She lied to me, the little devil. "You look just like everybody else, only shorter." So I got this self-image of "petite, small girl, feminine." That was okay. But I remember the day when I admitted that it just wasn't true. I was thirteen. Of course, even before that I must have known better, known that it wasn't true all along, because I would never look in the mirror. I have this black out in memories from thirteen to seventeen. I think things must have been so shitty that I pushed them away.

Anytime I was in an unfamiliar environment, I had to expect to get myself ready to be teased. Kids can be really, really cruel. It's hard to be an adult and try to be sensible about it when it's happening. Even though you know, whatever, "they're kids," or "they don't know better," whatever, it's hard. Even now I sometimes take action to avoid kids. Yesterday, in fact, I crossed the street to avoid a group of kids—there were just too many of them on the corner and I didn't want to deal with it, just in case.

I never used to date when I was younger. I had one date with this other disabled guy. My mother was like praying or something: "Oh, isn't it wonderful! Charlie going to come over again?" "I don't like Charlie, Mom." Charlie's father was thinking about how we could manage together. After one date—wait a minute!

I just never thought about dating and marriage. I felt it was out of the question. I thought boys would not be attracted to me. My first husband really had to chase me.

I was married for two and a half years in New York. My husband was disabled, too; the same disability. The disability had a lot to do with our getting married in the first place. We met and, well, I think we both felt we were each other's last chance.

For a while after I moved to Berkeley, and realized that there were non-disabled men interested in me, I think my attractions were toward pretty conventionally "good looking" men. That was a big thing: I could do better than a cripple. God that's hard to admit. I don't have that anymore, thank goodness, but for a while it certainly was like that. Like, from never doing anything but a cripple to never again.

It wasn't until about a year ago that I really knew what I looked like. If I ever looked at myself in a full-length mirror (which I never did), I would get freaked out. I couldn't understand how people could relate normally to someone who looked like that. It was also that, until real recently, I was never around people who had my disability. So I just didn't know what I looked like. And what I look like really looks so different.

About a year ago, I went into therapy, because who wants that shock every time you pass a department store window. I just needed to integrate what I really look like with who I am. You don't want to be confronted with your physical difference all the time. But the shock is enough to kill you if you keep hiding from it.

A friend of mine goes to Little People of America conventions. I despise that name, incidentally. It's so cutesy. She said you walk into the convention hall and see 500 others like you. It is a shock at first: "Do I look like this? Do I look like that one? Oh god, I don't want to look like this." And then you snap out of it. I want to go to one of the conventions just to experience that sense of being in a place where everyone is like me.

I get really excited when I walk into a room full of disabled people, especially disabled women. Last weekend, I went to a disabled-only conference and it was terrific. Even seeing a couple of young disabled women who I knew hadn't quite worked things out about being disabled. They look so fragile. They were trying to look extremely feminine; looking to find someone to go to bed with, I'm sure. They didn't want to hang out with us, didn't want to be too closely identified with the other disabled women. They'll get over it.

There is a real hierarchy of what is acceptable appearance within the disabled community: what is beautiful, what is ugly. At the top is someone who sits in a wheelchair but looks perfect. I have a friend who has cerebral palsy; she always says cerebral palsy is the dregs. They drool and have a speech impairment, movement problems, that kind of thing. On the high end of the scale is the person with a polio disability because physically they look okay. It's something we have to work on.

I am personally working on trying to finally enjoy my appearance a little more. I want to play with clothes like I never have. If you don't look at yourself, you don't want to think about what you look like in your clothes. I'm trying to get out of that now. I found someone to sew for me—all my clothes have to be special made—and asked her to make me a dress. I don't wear dresses because of this shame about my legs. But now I think I will. It's time to play around a little more.

Paula
"I have to make some practical decisions related to getting older"

I guess I am "losing my looks" as I approach forty. I have to find a
new image of myself as an older attractive woman. I used to be real
"pretty"—I could play the coquette. But there is nothing more awful
than being a coquette and being older. It goes along with all those
funny things that don't look like a drag on younger women, but do on
older women.

You see an older woman with eye make-up piled on and a
shrunken mouth with the bigger outline in dark red lipstick—it looks
terrifying. And then if she is dressed all in pink and giggling too-oh
god. It's my image of a truly pathetic person. A younger woman could
get away with it though, all of it. At least some younger women can. I
could, I had those kind of looks, but I don't have them anymore. Or I
won't have them much longer, anyway. If I'm going to be a real
giggler, I only have a couple more years to do it in.

I got a lot of things when I was younger being a coquette, but as
you get older you can't use them anymore. It starts to look ridiculous. I
noticed in my last affair that there were real remnants of the coquette in
my behavior. The other woman was so clearly butch, so withdrawn,
playing up her masculine characteristics. That kind of personality asks
for something to fill it up; for someone to be light and silly and sweet.

All my old training came to the surface. It's always there when
you need it. It makes me even more uncomfortable when I switch it on
around men. Then it is acknowledging that they have power, and that I
recognize their power. I pay a certain homage to it if I act the coquette.

Certain kinds of clothes will make it less likely that I act that way.
If I wear utilitarian clothes, I'm in very little danger of being coquet-
tish. The more masculine my clothes, the less likely I am going to
surprise myself doing something I don't like. But it is awfully subtle. I
mean what is the difference between a giggle and a laugh?

No clothes feel right to me. If I'm dressed thoughtlessly, I feel
sloppy. If I dress neatly, with my sweater tucked in just so, I feel
preppy. There is no way I can win. There are so few outfits that I think
project that I am in two worlds; that I identify with the rebellious—
shall I say it?—younger people, and also with the "Other" people of
which I am becoming one.

I have the problem that if I'm too dressed up, I look like I stepped out of a women's magazine. You can't be 5'10", thin and even-featured and not look fashion identified if you dress up. So I always have to go backward from that image. Wearing make-up is a problem for me too. It tends to give me even more of a doll face.

I don't feel panicked about getting older. I went through that at twenty-seven or twenty-eight. You know, when you realize you aren't going to die before you're thirty and that you will go on and grow old. But now I feel like I have to make some practical decisions related to getting older: Do I wear make-up or not? Do I accept the way something looks or do I change it? Do I take out the gray in my hair or do I leave it? Those sorts of things.

My father always said that gray hair makes the lines in your face softer. Both my parents went gray young, and they both really liked it. So I internalized the value that gray hair is good. I've been watching my hair go gray and enjoying the silvery effect. And then I made the mistake of using henna on my hair and the gray disappeared. Now that it's gone, I feel like I'm pretending to be something I'm not—younger. I have the feeling that I robbed myself of the badge of maturity.

People your own age determine your standard of beauty, I've noticed. I look at someone who is twenty now and find them a little blank; they haven't developed depth and interest. Then I look at someone my own age, say thirty-five or forty, and I don't think of them as young or old. I think of them as being as they should be. Like me.

When I think of myself as the young, pretty coquette of yesteryear, a lot of my identity including my sexuality—my sense of "being good in bed"—is based on how I looked and how I reacted. But if I lose those things and refuse to be the aging coquette, I can't any longer be the person who lays back and lets things happen to her.

Adena

"I have to do what I am doing simply to get control of my life"

Since I was ten, I have fluctuated between ten and twenty-five pounds above a weight I would find comfortable. This year, I joined Overeaters Anonymous (OA). The first meeting I went to felt like a cross between human services people and the Moonies. Everybody there was talking the same lingo—"I really appreciate your sharing that with me. I am having a fantasy about you..." And being so supportive you could die. Still, I tried another meeting and that one was better.

It took a long time to get used to it all. The biggest problem for me has been that OA asks you to admit that you are powerless. Now for a feminist who has been struggling for how many years with power—to gain knowledge about power and to feel more personally powerful in the world as a woman—it is hard to come to OA and hear "you are powerless, say it, admit it and give it up."

For me, it has been a process of learning that I am powerless over a very specific thing, of learning to give up control of food. That does not mean I give up control in other areas.

My compulsiveness around food is clearly related to my sense of isolation. When I am not doing what I want with my life, food can be a real focus. I find that I do not compulsively overeat when involved in a relationship, or when am I going full strength doing political work. When I am out of the house, I lose weight because I am not wrapped up in food. So the question remains for me, do you go to OA when feeling compulsive about food or go organize around El Salvador?

You see, the danger is to say, "when I am involved with somebody or politically active, I am not a compulsive overeater." Because, in fact, I am. I am just not eating compulsively. That part is always there.

The OA position is that you can never stop it; they are not into a cure. They are not trying to discover why you are a compulsive overeater, they are just trying to help you manage it. Because if you are a compulsive overeater, you are constantly worrying about food—worrying while you are not eating about what you are going to eat and worrying while you are eating about what you have just eaten.

All this stuff comes from feeling really bad about yourself. People will say at meetings: "I was feeling really bad and I ate four bags of chocolate chip cookies..." Which comes first? I think it's feeling lousy about yourself that triggers the compulsive eating.

A lot of these women say they feel they are in a situation where they have no rights; no right to say what they need, to have their needs met, to tell other people to stop hurting them. So they eat. And then they feel guilty for being out of control and worried about being fat.

While the emphasis at OA is not size, everybody knows how much they've lost. There is a great amount of pride involved. Still the focus is not weight but managing compulsive behavior.

I sometimes feel very uncomfortable around really large women. Part of the time I think it is great because I feel so thin by comparison. But other times, I think if I am in a group of really large women, other people will see me as large too. I think I put off going to OA meetings in part because I thought I would be sitting in a room with 20 other people who all weighed 300 pounds. The idea really freaked me out. But I found that I was probably the largest. I don't think most of the women even started out at a really large size.

Having the name "compulsive overeating" on it helps. It reminds me that I am not alone; this is a problem other people have too. Where did feminism come from after all? Let us all know that we are not loony, that there is something out there doing something to us. I haven't worked out a structural analysis of compulsive overeating, but I do know there is a structure. It is not just me.

I think if we could break the link between body size and self-hatred, it would probably help the next generation of potential compulsive overeaters. But that's just not the only issue for those of us who are now compulsive about food. Virtually everyone at the meetings has been a compulsive overeater since they were children or teenagers.

So I'd say, do whatever you have to to change society, to change stuff around body image and beauty. But don't bother me right now because I have to do what I am doing simply to get control of my life. That is the bottom line.

Cathy

*"How can a woman with one breast match
how we are supposed to look?"*

———————

I knew I had cancer of the breast only twenty-four hours before
the operation. I had a biopsy done on a lump that neither my surgeon
not I expected to be cancer. When I woke up from the anesthesia he
simply said "do you want to do the mastectomy now or wait?"

As soon as I heard it was cancer, I knew I wanted to have it done
immediately. I didn't want to sit around and do research. I didn't want
to think about it. It wasn't so much fear—or at least it wasn't that I was
reacting out of fear. It was just that I had thought about it beforehand
and knew that if it was cancer I wanted it gone.

I had great support after the operation and, frankly, I think one of
the reasons is that I am a lesbian. I found that straight people were
much more threatened by me with one breast than were lesbians. Men
in particular seem threatened by "unwhole" women.

My doctor, the surgeon, was terribly upset by the idea that I was
not going to wear a prosthesis. The second day in the hospital, the day
after surgery, he starts talking to me about how I should have silicon
implants so I could look normal.

When I made it clear to him that I absolutely was not going to have
implants, he started telling me about buying a prosthesis. The only
good part was when he told me that the best place in the area to buy a
prosthesis is the Queen's Closet on Piedmont! It was the funniest damn
thing I had ever heard. He didn't get it, and I wasn't about to explain it
to him.

The oddest thing about this conversation was that there was
nothing I could say to silence him. He gently told me that he had seen
"many a marriage flounder on the shoals of a mastectomy." If I said "I
don't need this discussion because I am a lesbian" it would sound as if
lesbians don't care about how they look. I felt totally trapped listening
to him go on and on.

I never did get a prosthesis though. Why should I? For whom
would I wear something like that? I haven't worn a bra since my last
child was born, so I'd have to go out and buy all this expensive
underwear and a false tit. And a prosthesis is not cheap, incidentally.
They cost several—as in six or seven—hundred dollars. And the only
reason to do it would be to keep people from being threatened by
anyone looking physically different.

One out of every ten women gets breast cancer at some time in her life. There are a lot of people walking around out there with only one tit. It is good for people to know that it happens, to know it can happen to young people, to know that you don't necessarily die from it.

In the beginning, I decided that I wasn't going to do anything different; that I was going to wear exactly the same clothes as I had before. I've changed that. I've sort of softened my position on shocking people. When I go swimming, I do wear my two piece bathing suit. And, yes, it looks really weird. But that is my bathing suit—and that is my body. On the street though, I don't wear really revealing clothes anymore. It makes me feel too self-conscious. I guess that's what I've done: I've made compromises on how self-conscious I am willing to feel.

Constantly confronting sexism is exhausting. You can't do it non-stop. So you make compromises. But I make compromises to make myself comfortable, not other people. It is either their reactions or my feelings. I'm not willing to try to make other people less uncomfortable with the fact that I have had cancer and have one breast. Why the hell should I take care of them? I'm the one whose feelings should be protected.

The mastectomy has actually helped free me from worrying about other people's ideas of how I should look. I used to worry that I was fat and ugly. I always thought I should lose weight. Now I really feel like I don't have to use those standards—I mean how can a woman with one breast try to match those ideas put out about how we are supposed to look? I can't. I can't play the game anymore and that's been very good.

My self-image was much worse during the fourteen years that I was a "normal" two-breasted married woman. I felt much less sexually attractive than I do now. One of the nice things about being a lesbian is that all the rules are so much more relaxed (though they certainly are not gone).

When you violate the norm of having your sexuality determined by men, you are freeing yourself from such a major thing it is only natural to begin to free yourself from other things as well. At least, that is how it felt to me. I began to question everything. All the rules.

The mastectomy hasn't really affected my sexuality though my lover and I both were afraid it would. One night just after the operation, I woke up and she was crying. She was afraid that she wasn't going to be attracted to me anymore. It turned out that it was not a problem, but she had been afraid that it could be.

Deena

Photo: Hella Hammid

When I went in to get the bandages off, I took her and another friend with me for support. I had never seen a mastectomy scar and had no idea what my chest was going to look like. I was worried.

First of all, the surgeon made me wait twenty minutes—if I had been in there alone waiting for the unveiling of my new chest I would have been a nervous wreak. Fortunately my friends were there. Finally, one of them said, "let's just take a look and see what it's like." So I did. I looked at it and it wasn't that bad. And then, because I couldn't quite get the bandage loose—and wouldn't have known what to do with it if I had—I sort of put it back on.

When the surgeon came in, he was upset that two other people were with me. "You will have to wait outside, ladies." "No. I asked them to be here." I wish I could remember his exact reply, but what he said was something like "this is going to be so horrible that your guests might faint and I'll be too busy to take care of them." You can imagine how that would have felt if I hadn't already looked and known what to expect.

Kathryn

*"For me acne was the most ugly, obscene word
in the language"*

I was the only feminist I knew who had acne. I just had to find out
if there was anybody else who felt like me. About five years ago, I wrote
an anonymous letter to the British feminist magazine *Spare Rib*
expressing my distress and utter shame.

> ...I don't need to be pretty...I just wish I could do something
> about this acne which hurts me so much as it destroys the
> tissues of my skin, and which twists me inside as it destroys my
> self-regard, my confidence, my peace of mind, and worst of all,
> my love for my normal-skinned sisters...*

I got dozens of replies, all supportive, relating experiences very
similar to my own. It was an absolute revelation. I then wrote to a
dozen traditional women's magazines and asked them to put in a little
announcement urging women who had had acne to write me. Only
three magazines were prepared to do so; all the others wrote back and
said "we all know that it is terribly distressing, my dear, but it's just not
an issue that is important to our readers." Though, of course, in the
very next issue there would be yet another article on "how to have
clearer, smoother skin."

From the announcements that were run, I received nearly two
thousand letters. Reading them brought back every painful incident of
my own twelve year struggle. But it was also ultimately cathartic. I
was no longer alone. The letters were painfully familiar, our experiences so similar.

I didn't have teenage acne. My skin only started to get bad when I
was eighteen years old. Like most people I assumed that my acne was
caused by what I was eating, so I started to carefully watch my diet.
Every article and most medical people proclaim food to be an enemy. It
is no longer nutritious or enjoyable, it is the cause of one's acne. The
first time a woman reads that she must avoid certain food, she does. It
makes no difference. Then she hears that a different one holds the key.
So she rejects that one. Still no difference. She stops eating them
both—no effect. She stoically gives up more and more foods, yet sees
little improvement. By this time she is completely confused and at a
loss, terrified of eating half the things in the English diet and guilty
when one slips past her lips. "You must give up eating butter, sweets,

---

*Spare Rib, No. 89, December 1979.

biscuits, fruit, milk, oils, meat, ice cream, bread, cream, cakes, cheese, spices, nuts, crisps, shellfish, onions, chocolate, sugar..." She determines to exclude all the bad ones.

The pattern is of course familiar: deprivation causes cravings, clandestine consumption of more than you would normally eat, followed by overwhelming guilt and self-hate, and the resolution to never touch them again. It is no wonder that the majority of the women who wrote me were compulsive eaters and/or anorexic. Food assumes a power in the acne sufferer's life that is all out of proportion. It is the temptor and the punisher. It also assuages the anguish and anesthetizes the pain.

So eating for me was charged with significance. I was guiltily using food for solace and extra support, and I was getting fat. Maybe there was even a part of me that wanted to make myself fat and ugly because I couldn't stand the way men were treating women who were pretty.

As a teenager I had had seven years of solid girls-only education, very academic and very, very good. I suppose that was where I learned to expect that women's voices were heard, that women were intelligent, and that all paths were open to women. So I was totally unprepared for the co-educational reality of higher education. I went to university the same year my adult acne started. It was a total culture shock: lecture after lecture where men were listened to and women weren't. Where women were judged by their beauty not their ideas. There were so many things happening to me at the same time, and eating was a part of my response.

Another reason I became fat was that, because of my acne, I felt I didn't deserve a place in the world, that I was too ugly to be entitled to be angry or nasty or to react the way I really felt about things anymore. "People already hate me because I am repulsive so I've got to be a nice person. I've got to learn to be nice." In order to quell all those feelings of anger, I ate.

Every day was a battle in two ways—a battle against my body shape but more especially against my face. There were times when I became thin and my body looked conventionally attractive. But if I tried to wear nice clothes, I felt I became a complete anomaly. I would get these awful come-ons from men in the street, and if I would turn around, I could see the shock on their faces when they saw the state of my skin.

Clothes were a burden. Attractive, fashionable ones drew attention, and my purpose in life was to hide. But indifferent clothes implied a lack of effort, and seemed to suggest that my ravaged skin must also be the result of carelessness.

When my skin got bad, I went from being a socially popular teenager to a young woman without boyfriends for years. I see now that I contributed to my own isolation—something I couldn't have admitted to myself even a couple of years ago. I did have approaches from really nice men, but just felt that I was so ugly nobody could possibly fancy me; nobody could ever want to be near me, or like me, ever. I felt I didn't deserve to have boyfriends, and I certainly didn't deserve any enjoyable physical experiences.

I had been living with the man I am now married to for nearly a year before I let him see my bare face. One night I walked into the room without covering my face in make-up. My skin was in particularly bad shape. I burst into tears and said "I can't go on with a face like this." "A face like what?" he asked. So I went under the light: "look." But I couldn't raise my head. Finally I lifted my face to the light. "Oh. What is it?" I could not say the word acne. For me it was the most ugly, obscene word in the language. So I said "spots, I've got spots."

He was dead sympathetic: "you know, there is a very good article in *Spare Rib* about them." It was my anonymous piece. It's been a big subject in our marriage ever since. That is something I feel a little ambivalent about because of the loss of romance, I suppose. It was my ultimate dirty secret and he knows it. But of course his support has been so important. And you do need support to cope with the disease.

Acne is horrible physically. There are so many little things you have to do; constantly putting on these stupid creams or whatever the latest cure is from your dermatologist. The combination of painful treatment and self-contempt often leads to a pattern of self-punishment. You become completely alienated from your own body. You view it as an unpredictable thing out of control. You disown it. It does not deserve kindness or love. It deserves to be punished.

You start out with mild forms of pain inflicted on your skin: washing it in scalding water, ruthlessly applying the most searing creams a few times a day, devising your own strong applications of neat Dettol or vinegar. This, you understand, under the guise of efficacy—the skin needs to be as raw as possible if the creams are to penetrate and kill all those evil germs. The more it stings, the better it works. Of course the skin gets worse and then the real persecution begins.

You sit with a magnifying mirror right up to your face, forcing yourself to see this hideous spectacle—yourself. In desperation, women try to slice them off with razor blades, to dissolve them with concentrated peroxide, even to burn them off with cigarette ends.

All this is at a time when the disease is at its worst, at a time when, with any other disease, you would feel justified in being treated gently, being taken care of. Creams and lotions for accidents and other skin ailments are balms; they imply that the patient's body—and thus the patient—needs soothing and comforting. Acne creams are severe; they sear the blemished skin and shrivel hands and eyelids.

I used to go to a hospital for what was euphemistically called "sunlight treatments." But it was complete burning off of about three layers of skin and terribly painful. I would go under a lamp for about ten minutes and then, for a few hours afterwards, my skin would just burn and burn and burn.

By the end of that day or overnight, hundreds of tiny blisters came out. They would last about a day—you can't wash it, you can't touch it. Your face is absolutely bright red. Then the color would fade and I would look very, very tanned for about two days. But I couldn't move my face because it became like leather. And then it cracked, would you believe it? It just cracked and peeled off.

I went through these treatments in part because it helped but also because it was my punishment. "You are a revolting person, you deserve this pain as punishment." The skin would peel off the day or so before the new treatment—and it would begin all over again. I went through this for one entire year.

When my acne started I began wearing face make-up for the first time: powder and foundation. It became absolutely vital. I used to experiment with various kind of face make-up. No, that is the wrong word, not experiment. The whole thing was so clandestine. I could never go to a counter and ask their advice, like other people do, because the first things they would say was "well, obviously you need our astringent for your acne." And you couldn't say, "but I have tried everything, you don't understand, there is genuinely nothing I can do about it except cover it up." So I used to buy things on the off chance.

Acne suggests you're not clean and don't care about how you look. However, one of my main problems with acne was that I thought it made me look unintelligent. "People think I am thick because I have acne." Everybody else seems to get rid of their teenage spots, and you can't. You obviously don't know how to wash your face. Even me, god help me, if I see a girl with severe acne I don't expect her to be intellectual. Me!

I found my first teaching job hell because of my acne. I left all my jobs because of my skin. I would work until I would feel that my eccentric behavior was getting to be too noticeable—always rushing to the washroom to wash my face, never socializing with anyone, never going to the snack bar. I would start to feel that people thought I was weird and I couldn't tell them why. So I would leave.

Now that my face is much better, I am actually sticking to a job. I am on tablets now—sort of a guinea pig for a wonder drug which came over from the United States. Without it, I would certainly have acne now. There do appear to be some serious side effects from the medication. It may build up in your liver and kidneys, it quite possibly causes birth defects, and it makes your bones ache and gives you conjunctivitis.

But it is all worth it. Compared to acne, god, it is nothing. A few years ago, if somebody had said to me, "you can have a drug that will cure your acne but you will only live ten years, or you can live to be a hundred with your skin as it is," I would have taken the ten years.

Remember, for more than a decade I had severe acne. In that time, I changed radically, losing all those attributes I thought of as essentially me. I used to be an extrovert, fun loving, independent, a strong-willed person. In those twelve years, I lost confidence in myself, my self-image completely altered. I had been a reasonably pretty teenager, I suppose. I never had any lack of boyfriends or friends. Basically I had few problems with the way I looked.

Through the years of acne, I became somebody completely obsessed with the way she looked every minute of the day. I even dreamt about acne. I became somebody who hated herself so deeply that suicide was a real possibility for nearly six years.

Some of my loss of confidence isn't just the result of the years of acne. It seems to me to be more general, a part of growing up for women. As women get older they seem often to lose their self-confidence, whereas men become more confident. I may never be the self-confident girl I once was, because of sexism as well as the acne, but I am on my way. The one thing it does give you if you do survive, is a certain strength and an incredible insight into other women.

I am still feeling my way with looking more "attractive." It is literally only in the last year that my weight and skin have stabilized. I bitterly regret the loss of the years eighteen to thirty, and the loss of the person I would have been, the sexuality I would have discovered.

But those are gone and now I am slowly coming into my own. I've started buying clothes that are attractive, even vaguely fashionable. But I also feel guilty in some way because of the women in my office.

They are all middle aged and struggling with weight, menopause and the loss of their "attractive youth." They are constantly going on about how lucky I am to be so thin, so young, so attractive. I feel I want to explain to them all, "I haven't always been like this, honestly. I am a compulsive eater and I have had awful years of being a hermit." But I don't say anything. I know what they mean.

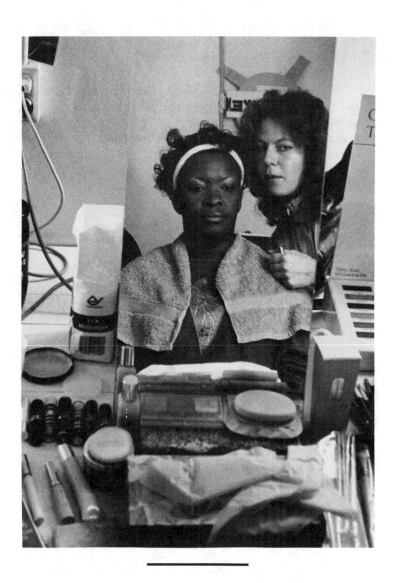

2
Skin
Deep

"Mirror, mirror on the wall, who is the fairest of them all?" As children we accept that "the fairest" is the same sort of measure as the fastest, the tallest or the richest. Later, in the growing sophistication of adulthood, we determine that the most beautiful is more like the bravest, the most popular or the most powerful. It becomes a judgement about which one might have an *opinion* but remains a quality that ultimately can be established by an independent and attentive authority. "Ladies and Gentlemen, the judges have reached a decision. The new Miss World is...."

Adults thus continue to pose the question "who is the fairest" as though it were meaningful, even when the category of "them all" includes women of diverse races and nationalities. Indeed female beauty is becoming an increasingly standardized quality throughout the world. A standard so strikingly white, Western and wealthy it is tempting to conclude there must be a conscious conspiracy afoot.

But in fact no hidden plot is needed to explain the pervasiveness of this image. The fantasy of the Good Life populated by Beautiful People wearing The Look has seized the imagination of much of the world. This Western model of beauty represents a mandate for a way of life for women throughout the world regardless of how unrelated to each of our ethnic or economic possibilities it is. We invest a great deal in the fantasy, perhaps all the more, the further we are from being able to attain it. This international fantasy becomes the basis of our myths of eroticism, success and adventure.

It is "Charlie's Angels" (women on a 1970s U.S. TV show) who appear to have a good time in the world, not women who are fat or small or dark-skinned. As the center of a world economic system, the U.S. owns the biggest share of the global culture machine. By entering that world in imagination, each woman aims to be whiter, more

37

Western, more upper class. This goes beyond simple manipulation.

While the Hearst Corporation is trying to maximize profits on a global scale, that does not fully explain *Cosmopolitan's* popularity in seventeen languages around the world. The Cosmo package seems to offer everything: sexuality, success, independence and beauty. It is powerful and compelling. A woman working all day making microchips who buys lipstick or cigarettes is buying some tiny sense of dignity and self-esteem along with the glamour.

In large part, the content of the global image is determined by the mechanics of the sell: who creates the images for what products to be marketed through which media controlled by whom? The beauty trade (cosmetics, toiletries, fragrance and fashion) is expanding its market worldwide. And a world market means global marketing. For instance, during the Christmas season of 1982, the same commercials for Antaeus and Chanel No. 5 perfumes were being used throughout Europe, the U.S. and Latin America.[1] And in 1985, *Business Week* reported that Playtex had kicked off:

> ...a one ad fits all campaign...betting that a single marketing effort can sell a new bra around the world...At one point several years ago, Playtex had 43 versions of ads running throughout the world with local managers in charge...This year Playtex gave all its world wide business to New York's Grey Advertising.[2]

Tony Bodinetz, vice-chair of KMP in London (a division of the huge international advertising corporation Saatchi and Saatchi) believes this kind of advertising campaign arises in part from cultural chauvinism:

> The use of the same ad in various countries is in part based on a calculation of cost effectiveness, but partly it is simply a reflection of an attitude of mind. Some company executive in Pittsburg or Los Angeles or somewhere thinks "if it works in Pittsburg it'll work in London...why the hell would they be any different?" One of the things we fight against here is the fact that American solutions are often imposed on us.[3]

Bodinetz appears to be a minority voice in a company committed to just such a global advertising strategy: "They are committed to it because they need to be. They are looking to get those huge world clients and the way to get the clients is to sell this concept, so they have to believe it," says Bodinetz. The competition among the advertising giants for the large corporate accounts is intense. And the world of multinational product and image is very small indeed.

About a dozen advertising agencies worldwide represent the majority of major multinational corporations and themselves operate across national boundaries.[4] The number three advertising agency in the U.S., J. Walter Thompson, for example, is also the most important agency in Argentina, Chile and Venezuela, number two in Brazil and ABC—the American Broadcasting Corporation—a private television these global image makers are American advertising agencies. The products they hype are also overwhelmingly American. U.S. companies alone account for nearly half of global expenditures on advertising, outspending the closest rival, Japan, by five to one. Small wonder then that advertising images tend to be recognizably North American.[5]

These global advertising campaigns increasingly ignore national differences in determining the products to be marketed and the images used to sell them. The ads contribute to the belief that success and beauty are brand names with a distinctly white American look to them. Trade journals *Advertising Age* and *Business Abroad* note the trend: "Rubinstein Ads not Altered for Señoras;" "World Wide Beauty Hints: How Clairol Markets Glamour in Any Language."

The advertising agency Saatchi and Saatchi is enthusiastic about "world branding" and global culture:

> Market research will be conducted to look for similarities not seek out differences. Similarities will be exploited positively and efficiently...developing advertising for an entire region of the world, and not simply for one market to find a real advertising idea so deep in its appeal that it can transcend national borders previously thought inviolate.[6]

Western corporations are not alone in pursuing this transcendent advertising ideal. Shiseido, the Japanese giant in cosmetics, has recently revamped its advertising to present a "determinedly international thrust."[7] "It is easy to create an ordinary, nice picture with a nice model and a nice presentation for the product," explains a company executive, "but we wanted to be memorable without being too realistic. Realism would have too closely defined our market." Shiseido hints at its Asian origin—"intrigue from the Orient"—but its models are white and its targeted market is "the international affluent elite."[8] Saatchi and Saatchi agrees that this is the strategy of the future:

> Are social developments making outmoded the idea that the differences between nations with regard to this or that durable, cosmetic or coffee were crucial for marketing strategy? Con-

sumer convergence in demography, habits and culture are
increasingly leading manufacturers to a consumer-driven
rather than a geography-driven view of their marketing
territory...Marketers will be less likely to tailor product
positioning to the differing needs of the country next door and
more likely to operate on the basis of the common needs for
their products.[9]

A "consumer-driven" view of marketing means focusing on that
segment of any society likely to purchase a given product. For many
products, in particular luxury items, the potential market in large parts
of the world remains extremely limited. It is certainly true that
members of these national elites often more closely resemble their
counterparts in other countries than they do their own less affluent
compatriots.

In turn, the upper class serves as the model of success and glamour
for the rest of the nation. All the pieces of the picture begin to fit neatly
together, confirming that there is but one vision of beauty. The
woman on the imported American television program resembles the
woman in the Clairol ad resembles the wife of the Prime Minister or
industrial magnate who dresses in the latest French fashion as faithfully
reported in the local version of *Cosmopolitan*.

Corporate advertising is not, then, uniquely responsible for the
homogenization of culture around the world. But it is an important
team player. Tony Bodinetz explains:

> I don't think you can just point the finger and blame
> advertising, because advertising never leads. But admittedly it
> is very quick to sense what is happening on the streets or
> around the world and to jump on a bandwagon. Of course
> while it is true that advertising never sets the pace, it cannot
> escape its share of the responsibility for confirming the view
> that to "join the club" you've got to look like this, smell like
> this, speak like this and dress like this.[10]

This vision of beauty and success has been made familiar around
the world not only through ads but via the American media of
magazines, television and motion pictures. In much of the world, a
large portion of television programming is composed of American
imports. Foreign programs make up well over half of television fare in
such countries as Ecuador, Chile and Malaysia.[11] In Western Europe,
the Middle East and parts of Asia more than 20 percent of all television
programs are made in the U.S. One popular American program,
"Bonanza," was once seen in 60 countries with an estimated audience

of 350 million. The contemporary equivalent, "Dallas," is watched by millions from Malaysia to South Africa.[12]

The Americanization of the world media has had useful spinoffs for marketing. Saatchi and Saatchi again:

> ...television and motion pictures are creating elements of shared culture. And this cultural convergence is facilitating the establishment of multinational brand characters. The world wide proliferation of the Marlboro brand would not have been possible without TV and motion picture education about the virile rugged character of the American West and the American cowboy, helped by increasing colour TV penetration.[13]

That American television should be so omnipresent is not entirely due to chance or to the excellence of the U.S. "sitcom." In the 1950s, ABC—the American Broadcasting Corporation, a private television company, received U.S. government AID funding to create the first television stations in Ecuador, Colombia and Peru. They also provided technical assistance for the development of many others. By the early 1970s, ninety countries throughout the world were buying ABC programs and business agreements between ABC and its Latin American affiliates allow the corporation to choose both programs and sponsors for peak viewing hours.[14] Even without such direct control, foreign imports are often the programming of choice because small local networks find it much cheaper to buy American programs than to produce their own.

Television, and the related Hollywood film industry, are not the only media plying their wares around the world. Many of the top twenty American magazine corporations also produce for a world market. Hearst Corporation, the third largest magazine corporation in the U.S., produces a Latin American version of "Good Housekeeping"—*Buenhogar*—and *Vanidades* (the women's magazine with the largest circulation in Latin America). Hearst also publishes the internationally popular *Cosmopolitan*. Conde Nast, number six on the U.S. list, publishes and distributes adapted versions of *Vogue* magazine in many countries.[15]

Researchers in Latin America studied the content of these transnational women's magazines and found striking similarities from country to country. The majority of articles focused on beauty, fashion or products for use in the home. Perhaps even more telling, almost a third of the total space was devoted to advertising and 60 percent of all advertisements were for the products of transnational corporations.[16]

Of course, the media have always relied heavily on advertising. Now, though, the relationship is so intimate that one corporation may own both the magazine advertising a product and the company producing it. Media authority Ben Bagdikian puts it bluntly: "The major media and giant corporations have always been allies; they are now a single entity."[17]

Four of the fifty largest U.S. media corporations are among the fifty largest advertisers. All three of the major American television networks and three of the four leading movie studios are part of companies so large that they appear on the list of the 500 largest corporations in the United States.[18] Thus, not only does one country determine the jingle much of the world will hum, but a very few, large corporations own the piper.

While it would be wrong to suggest that this is the result of a conscious conspiracy among the various parts of the global culture machine (U.S.-based multinational corporations, U.S.-dominated international advertising and the U.S. entertainment and media industries) it is safe to say that they all benefit from a collective global fantasy of success and beauty defined by white skin, Western culture and imported products.

> Elaborate make-up is part of the electronics image in Malaysia, and the factories even provide classes in how to apply it. This allows the workers to feel they are part of a global culture which includes the choice between Avon and Mary Quant products.[20]
>
> There just seems to be a great desire to aspire to Western values and Western culture...Often an ad will be written in English because that is one way of flattering the audience: "You are smart, sophisticated and educated." I suppose that is also why the models tend to be white...[21]
>
> ...Dr. Fu Nong Yu [a plastic surgeon in Peking] performs "eye jobs" to create folded or "double" eyelids, considered a mark of wide-eyed beauty...Most northern Chinese are born without double eyelids and Fu takes a few stitches to remove the epicanthal fold in the upper eyelid that is typical of Asians...[22]
>
> Japanese television commercials are a paean to the American way of life, full of glamorous movie stars and famous sports heroes...Despite a growing pride in things Japanese, the United States remains a cultural pacesetter for Japan...If a Japanese company cannot find an American celebrity to endorse its

product, it may opt for displaying the product in a recognizably U.S. setting or placing a blue-eyed, blond model
alongside it.[23]

Naturally, this trend toward global cultural homogenization has
not gone unchallenged. Indigenous culture remains a powerful alternative to the white Western model of success and beauty. In some
countries, traditional images are officially promoted as a response to
the flood of imported Western culture. In other countries, local culture
acts subversively as the bearer of otherwise illegal messages of political,
economic and cultural resistance.

Following the Sandinista victory over the Somoza dictatorship in
Nicaragua, sexist advertising was banned. If a woman now appears in
an advertisement, there must be a reason other than providing a sexual
come-on to the potential buyer. While *Vanidades* and *Cosmopolitan*,
with their transnational advertising, can still be purchased in Managua,
the local billboards do not offer images of the wealthy white glamour
girl.

Another, although very different reaction to Western sexualized
imagery of women, is evidenced in the Islamic countries of North
Africa and the Middle East. A dramatic symbol of religious, national
and patriarchal culture, the veil, is increasingly being adopted by
women in these countries. The use of the veil to reclaim (and in some
cases to re-invent) indigenous culture is clearly problematic but hardly
inexplicable. Shortly before the overthrow of the Shah in Iran, the
most popular women's magazine in that country was *Zan-e Ruz*
(*Woman of Today*) with a circulation of over 100,000. The periodical
was filled with love stories starring blonde, blue-eyed heroines lifted
directly from Western magazines. Of the 35 percent of the periodical
taken up with ads, much focused on beauty and cosmetic products
again often featuring blonde models. One researcher observed "the
great stress on physical appearance in a situation of acute sexual
repression is...somehow ironic."[24] More than ironic, the resulting
tensions may have helped encourage both the Islamic revival and the
subsequent return to the veil.

Significantly, while the veil may be an important and visible
symbol of resistance to Western culture and values, it is worn by
women only. Women throughout the world tend to be designated as
culture bearers and given the burdensome responsibility of preserving
traditional values and aesthetics. In recent studies in several African
countries, researchers discovered that women were seen both as
repositories of traditional culture and those most likely to succumb to

Western influences. Women in Uganda, for example, were seen as:

> ...scapegoats not only for male confusion and conflict over
> what the contemporary roles of women should be, but for the
> dilemmas produced by adjusting to rapid social change. Where
> men have given up traditional customs and restraints on dress,
> but feel traitors to their own culture, they yearn for the security
> and compensation of at least knowing that women are loyal to
> it.[25]

In much the same way, women in Zambia have been held
responsible "when the state of morality was chaotic..." and when
cultural traditions became "contaminated by Western influence."[26]
Unfortunately, women of the Third World singlehandedly can no
more turn back Western cultural domination than they can be held
responsible for its powerful and enduring influence. And while women
certainly *are* at the forefront of many forms of resistance including the
cultural, "tradition" may not be the only element women will choose
to draw on in creating a culture that speaks of and to their lives.

At the international festival of women's culture, Black women fill
the stage night after night with their presence. To watch them is not
simply to admire but to feel pride. They allow for no less. Their
self-respect is utterly contagious and offers a vision of power beyond
the borders of white commercial culture.

These women using music, language and movement different
from my own, still speak directly to me. "This is a heart beat. This is all
of our heart beats. And it is beating for you. And for you. And for
you." (Edwina Lee Tyler playing her African drum.)

The destructive effect of racism on the self-image of people of
color[27] is well-documented and much bemoaned—especially among
anti-racist whites. Isn't it terrible that Blacks have felt a need to "relax"
their curly hair to appear more attractive? Isn't it shocking that eye jobs
creating a Western eyelid were popular among certain Vietnamese
women during the war? Isn't it distressing that the model for female
beauty sold to developing nations is the same White Woman sold to the
West?

Yes. But at some level it is also profoundly reassuring to white
women; we are, after all, the model. We do embody at least one element
of the beauty formula. Our white Western lives are the stuff of global
fantasy and demonstrably enviable.

This international commercial trend can easily be misrepresented
as evidence of a unanimous esthetic judgement. But people of color
are not alone in buying fantasies packaged in a distant ethnic reality.

For the Western white, "paradise is tropical, and passion, rhythmic movement and sensuality all wear dark skin. Just as the white Western world serves as the repository for certain elements of a global myth of success and beauty, so too does the world of color represent related myths of sensuality, adventure and exoticism.

The fantasy of the Western Good Life is grounded in the reality of the economic privilege of the industrialized West. Perhaps the fantasy of sensuality and passion ascribed to the Third World refects something similar about the realities of privilege and oppression. It is certainly true that to maintain a position of privilege in a world of tremendous poverty requires some measure of emotional shutting down, a distancing of the self from the unentitled other. Puerto Rican poet Aurora Levins Morales suggests that this has consequences for white culture:

> There is a kind of aliveness that has been obtained in oppressed cultures that gets shut down in dominant culture. There is a lot of fear that comes with privilege. Fear that others want to take your stuff away from you. It means an incredible locking down. Also you have to be in control all the time. Being always in control is not conducive to sensuality.[28]

Power is the arbiter determining which characteristics will be ascribed to the self and which will be projected onto the other. These complimentary images are the basis of myths of white and black, male and female, the self and Other.

———

"Wendy Chapkis" has never been an easy name. While Wendy was okay as a child in its unobtrusive Americanness, the permanent diminutive annoyed me as I grew older. Chapkis was even more difficult. It lent itself far too easily to the distortions of which children are so fond; chapped lips being the grade school favorite. And it hasn't exactly rolled off the tongue in any place I've ever lived.

But all along, I knew there was something more basic making me uncomfortable. Wendy is as WASPy as *Peter Pan*; Chapkis is all Russian Jew. My last name longed to be spoken in a thickly accented tongue by the sort of people with whom my first name might not mix. The hybrid name is a gift of my red-headed Norwegian Lutheran mother and my dark curly haired Russian Jewish father. Even in the land of the melting pot, mixed heritage bothers people; a feeling given voice every time someone has felt compelled to tell me "but you don't

look Jewish." Ethnicity is supposed to be distinct and visible.

Anti-semitic observations frequently have been shared with me because no one "suspects" that a blonde, blue-eyed Wendy isn't comfortably one-of-us.

Over the years, I have learned to like my names. Together. They remind me that separating the self from the ethnic Other is not only potentially dangerous but ultimately schizophrenic.

———

Before the colonial experience of the eighteenth and nineteenth centuries, most non-European societies were viewed with fear by the white West. Contact was seen as dangerous. But from the powerful position of colonizer over the colonized, curiosity about "exotic peoples" joined, if not entirely replaced fear of them. According to anthropologist Deborah Root, in the colonial period:

> Europeans accentuated the differences between their own and other societies to artificially create "mystery" for the sake of aesthetic and emotional sensation...The use of exotic imagery directed attention away from the question of power and European dominance, in effect normalizing the colonial situation...Power permitted the European to selectively idealize fragments of native culture while systematically destroying the society as a whole.[29]

The colonized world thus became more than a testing place for European manhood, it became a necessary counterpoint to the white male self. Similarly, sexualized images of Black women "freed" white European women to serve as models of purity for white men. The "exotic native," male and female, was created and defined by the white colonizer, much as he created the boundaries of his new colonial possessions. Neither had any necessary relationship to precolonial history, culture or identity. But through the creation of the colonial Other, the imperial self was given definition.

The division between the white self and Black Other was not as solid as the colonial mind would have had it. Not only did the colonized refuse to passively accept their assigned parts, but the secret self projected onto the non-European Other remained powerfully attractive to the colonizer himself. The fear of "going native" rivaled the fear of native revolt. The creation of the colonial self and its disintegration into the native other is perhaps best described in Joseph Conrad's *The Heart of Darkness*. "He couldn't get away...he would remain; go off...disappear for weeks; forget himself amongst these people—forget himself—you know."[30]

The nearer the white self approaches the Black Other, the more blurred become the landmarks by which a "civilized" identity is created and maintained:

> ...what we could see was just the steamer we were on, her outlines blurred as though she had been on the point of dissolving...that was all. The rest of the world was nowhere, as far as our eyes and ears were concerned. Just nowhere. Gone, disappeared, swept off without leaving a whisper or a shadow behind.[31]

This fear of losing one's bearings and succumbing to the "passionate uproar" is the constant temptation of the sexualized Other.

Even in relations within a race, the powerful project onto the less powerful those aspects of the self which might conflict with maintaining control and privilege, such as non-instrumental passion or selfless nurturing. In *Heart of Darkness*, the brutality of the key figure Kurtz is complimented and facilitated by the innocence of his woman back home. His "intended" is the model of white purity: "this fair hair, this pale visage, this pure brow, seemed surrounded by an ashy halo from which the dark eyes looked out at me."[32] Her illusion that her man is good and noble is indispensible: "I believed in him more than anyone on earth...He needed me. I would have treasured every sigh, every word, every glance."[33]

In the polarized world of self and Other, no one really *sees* anyone else. White and Black, men and women, view each other as essentially foreign. The result is "the horror." The blind faith of the white woman gives moral purpose to her madman's deeds. The white man's creation of the savage gives him justification for "exterminating the brutes," the "criminals, enemies, rebels." The natives, among whom Kurtz "loses himself," turn him into the supreme Other, a god, plundering and murdering one another in his name.

Many contemporary Hollywood films rely on just this sort of stylized distinction between the self (most often a white male hero) and the Other (women and the Third World). True to form, the other becomes an exotic territory to be explored, consumed, rescued or conquered with little or no independent existence. In this genre, women are cast in vacuous roles where beauty and sex appeal are of the essence; the Third World is reduced to the physical beauty of a colorful setting and the dangerous sensuality of primitive passions.

Romantic adventure films can sometimes combine both elements by using a Third World locale as a travel poster backdrop against which a hero romances the woman of his dreams. It is often the case that the male hero is no more authentic than the woman and the romantic world built around him. But unlike them, he exists on his own. Everything and everybody else appear primarily as material with which he can construct a heroic identity.

Women and people of color are consequently limited to roles of romantic interest, helpless victim, evil foe or loyal sidekick. Most commonly, it is a white woman who is chosen to be the love object, often in conjunction with a role as damsel in distress. The role of villain (often considered too powerful for a woman) is commonly filled by disfigured, disabled or Third World men. The part of sidekick is also usually male since it suggests a sort of partnership (and male bonding) inappropriate between a woman and a hero. Since a sidekick ideally should be dispensible (a true hero needs no one) and not quite as much a man as the star, an Asian man servant, a comic Black man, a chimpanzee or a precocious child fit the bill nicely.

In film, women of color are only noticeable by their absence. Their roles are so marginal that they border on the invisible. When not altogether absent, these women tend to appear as silent servants or fleeting symbols of sexuality—exotic dancers, sorceresses, prostitutes. Women, Black and white, who do appear are almost never stars of their own adventures.

The limited representation of women and people of color in popular culture reinforces the idea that the world is a white man's playground; a fantasy sanitized to remove disturbing images of those who would dispute that claim to ownership. The industrialized West may still economically control large parts of the world, but gone is the colonial confidence that this is a stable arrangement based on mutually acknowledged natural superiority of white over Black.

Our celluloid fantasies may well be set in the sands of the Sahara, the lush vegetation of the Amazon or the jungles of the Dark Continent. But in reality the white West fears Arabs, Latinos, Blacks. By removing most of the troublesome natives from the landscape and domesticating those who remain, popular culture turns the countries of the Third World into interchangeable travel posters. These films depict the world in a similarly airbrushed fashion as men's magazines do their female models: any suggestion of imperfection or real danger as opposed to adventure is retouched and removed. Danger implies the possibility of hostility and failure; adventure only suggests the opportunity to successfully prove one's masculinity. The final product should never suggest that the country or woman on display is anything but inviting, available and welcoming. Or that white western men are anything but heroes.

One particularly popular recent film managed to combine virtually all these elements in the creation of the Superhero, Indiana Jones. *Indiana Jones and the Temple of Doom* is breathtaking in its out and out racism and sexism. Willy-the-White-Woman (the romantic interest) is the butt of an ongoing joke. She is a model of cultural insensitivity ("you are insulting them and embarrasing me," warns the hero), consumerism ("I was happy in Shanghai. I had a little house and a garden, my friends were rich and we went to parties all the time in limousines. I hate being outside...") and petty self-interest ("I burnt my fingers and cracked a nail," she explains as she tosses their only gun out the window during a shoot out). Obviously with such a female companion, Indiana Jones is in need of male assistance. This comes in the form of a relentlessly cute Asian boy.

While the hero is not only master of languages and cultural differences, but of white water, wild beasts and the forces of evil, Willy walks about the jungle in high heels, has no rapport with nature ("This place is completely surrounded by living things!" she shrieks), whines incessantly ("I hate the water and I hate being wet and I hate you") and stands helplessly by while her "men" (the child is more of an adult than she) take on the world.

This trio of Superhero, pint-sized Third World sidekick and their beautiful female burden arrive in an empoverished Indian village and are greeted as gifts from the gods: "We prayed to Siva to help us...it was Siva who made you fall from the sky so you will go to Pangkok palace, find the stone and bring it back." The starving villagers are at the mercy of an evil force—"There is a new maharaja and again the palace has the power of the dark light." The palace is guilty of spreading "darkness all over" the British colony.

Not surprisingly, the evil high priest at Pangkok shows little respect for the empire: "the British find it amusing to inspect us at their convenience...they worry so about their empire. Makes us all feel like well cared for children." While the film confirms that these Indians are indeed worthy of close inspection (for they are behaving very badly), the British just as clearly are not up to the task. It requires an American hero to make good on the promise of paternal protection. The white American duo, Indy and Willy, literally unshackle the children of the Third World, freeing them not from colonialism, but from their evil

Guy Laroche

le parfum
des paradis
retrouvés

Paris

dark-skinned masters. The British-led troops arrive after the fact to lend their support to the essentially single-handed heroism of white male America.

Women of color typically have no role in the adventure. Indeed golden haired, pale skinned Willy becomes the only Third World beauty around when she appears in full Indian dress at a banquet in Pangkok palace. This exotic white princess is in striking contrast to the only other women shown in the film—the supplicating and starving Indian mothers back in the village.

The all-male secret society of the Black palace worshippers has a powerful enough appeal that our hero, Indiana Jones, himself nearly succumbs. After being forced to become an initiate, the hero forgets himself and temporarily abandons woman and child. "Indy, for god's sake, help me," begs Willy. "What is the matter with you? Indiana help us! Please snap out of it. *You aren't one of them!* Please come back to us...don't leave me."

Unlike the Hollywood film industry, the world of advertising is a rich source of imagery of women of color, often combining racist and sexist stereotypes in one picture. Advertisements using Asian women, for example, are evocative not only of the sexual mystery but also the docility and subservience supposedly "natural to the oriental female." This is true whether the product is the woman herself (as an assembly line worker or a "hospitality girl" in a holiday "sex tour") or another good or service enhanced by the female touch. A Malaysian electronics firm advertising brochure reads:

> The manual dexterity of the oriental female is famous the world over. Her hands are small and she works fast with extreme care. Who, therefore, could be better qualified by nature and inheritance to contribute to the efficiency of the bench assembly line than the oriental girl?

And this from Thai International Airlines:

> Gentle people...caring for you comes naturally to the girls of Thai. The gentle art of service and courtesy is one they learn from childhood...Beautiful Thai.

As the advertising technique of "world branding" helps spread white Western culture to developing nations, Third World women increasingly appear in advertisements in the West promising entry to that vanishing world of the exotic. These women thus become metaphors for adventure, cultural difference and sexual subservience; items apparently increasingly hard to come by in the industrialized

East 東 Meets 逢 West 西

The new fall color collection from Ultima II

When Kipling said "never the twain shall meet" about East and West, he didn't have Ultima II to reckon with. This collection is Ultima's lyrical translation of the loveliest colors the Orient has to offer.

The copper of chrysanthemums, with a scrim of gold. The blushing pink of the inside of a shell. A deep peony shade. Colors like Imperial Fire, Garnet Moon, Silk Russet.

For your eyes, lips, cheeks and nails.

Starting early Autumn, *East Meets West*.

But only at your Ultima II Counter.

ULTIMA II

54

West.

Especially interesting are those ads selling travel and tourism. Their invitation is to escape to paradise on earth—in itself fascinating given the way Third World countries are represented in the other media. The split images are quite remarkable: the exotic is marketed as a holiday fantasyland while "the underdeveloped world" is used in the West as shorthand for poverty, hunger, political corruption and religious fanatacism.

Of course, airlines and other branches of the tourist industry, are in the business of selling fantasy not theories of underdevelopment. "A taste of Paradise to Sri Lanka...Discover the infinite beaches with the people of Paradise" whispers the Air Lanka ad. The text is set against a picture of a deserted white sandy beach with a small inserted photo of a smiling Asian flight hostess.

The use of foreign locales and peoples to enhance the magic properties of a product is an effective marketing technique. It is easier to suspend judgement and accept the promise of the fantastic if it is set far from familiar soil. Just as we doubt that the truly romantic can happen to people who look too ordinary, it is harder to believe that the truly fantastic can happen too close to home.

In the past, travel belonged to a small, very privileged elite. We saw pictures of Brigitte Bardot in St. Tropez and knew both were the stuff of dreams. Now we can choose to visit the Côte d'Azur on a holiday, taking advantage of bargain flights or package tours. But when we walk the streets of our collective dreams, we don't look like Bardot. And the romantic adventures that befell her seem to pass us by. Perhaps we are not beautiful enough, or rich enough, to bring out the true magic of St. Tropez?

Rather than concluding that the fantasy was never a full and true reflection of reality, we simply set our sights on ever more distant shores. The more inaccessible the better. Travel brochures almost always suggest that this spot is still "unspoiled"; perhaps the compulsive clicking of cameras is an attempt to recapture the quiet, frozen images of the dream we thought we bought. Back home, looking through the carefully composed shots, the exotic again resembles the airline ads that fed our fantasies.

Ironically, travel to exotic lands actually robs us of their exoticism; the exotic must remain unfamiliar in order to retain its mystery. Experience creates familiarity, something our culture teaches us is the antithesis of romance. So while travel ads promise access to the exotic, they must also emphasize its unknowable Otherness. A

Singapore Airlines ad reads: "Across four continents of the earth...you are an unsolved mystery in a *sarong kebaya*. Who are you Singapore Girl?"

A serenely beautiful Asian woman stares directly into the camera, an intimate look, steady and deep: "The airline with the most modern fleet in the world still believes in the romance of travel." And, as Singapore Airlines reminds us, there is nothing more romantic than the mysterious Asian woman. Nothing else appears in their ads. Exotic cloth is wrapped around undemanding oriental gentleness: "Enjoy the kind of inflight service even other airlines talk about, with gentle hostesses in sarong kebayas caring for you as only they know how." Yes, their girls have a reputation, but they don't mind.

Hilton International promotes their hotels in Hong Kong, Jakarta, Kuala Lumpur, Manila, Singapore, Taipei and Tokyo with the picture of five Asian women (some dressed in traditional outfits, others in Western service uniforms): "Life oriental style...A carefully melded crossroads of East and West. You've focused on Hilton International. A unique blend of Oriental hospitality and international service."

The ad speaks to the fantasy and the *fear* of travel in exotic lands. Hilton will help smooth out the cultural confusions by carefully melding East and West. A safe way to enjoy exoticism. You can "enter a world where a myriad of surrounding sights and sensations tantalize your imagination, and let the Hilton International world of thoughtful services *put your mind at ease.*" The hotel is no simple place to sleep, no more than an airline is simply a means of transportation. It is a fantasy, indeed A Way of Life, or at least the safe imitation of one. "Specializing in the unexpected—a lobby in exact replica of a sultan's palace. Our own cruising replica of a pirate chasing brigantine..."

Perfumes, cosmetics and certain fashion lines promise the look of the exotic for those unable or unwilling to actually travel to distant countries. The Ultima II cosmetic line by Revlon is marketed as a way for East to meet West. "The collection is Ultima's lyrical translation of the loveliest colors the Orient has to offer." Note the use of the word orient in so many of these ads. Orient is a realm of fantasy; Asia is a real life place. Orient brings to mind the mystery of the exotic region of the East; Asia says Vietnam, Red China, Toyota car competition. The most striking thing about the Ultima II "East Meets West" advertisement is the photograph accompanying it. Lauren Hutton sits on a cushion wearing something reminiscent of a kimono (but showing too much flesh). She looks down with a slightly amused smile at her hands folded in her lap. Across from her, an Asian woman dressed in a real kimono bows to this symbol of daring Western womanhood. This is apparently the proper attitude for East when meeting West.

Perfume ads are particularly fond of the exotic motif. And here again the racial stereotypes and the promise of exotic fantasy reign: "Island Gardenia by Jovan: Delicate. Exotic. Above all...Sensuous. Only in the islands do the most delicate flowers grow a little wilder." "Fidji by Guy Laroche: Fidji, le parfum des paradis retrouvés." "Mitsouko by Guerlain: Serenely mysterious..."

Even such a mundane product as panty hose can be sold with a touch of the exotic: "The look...the feel...of the Orient. Now yours in a pantyhose. Sheer Elegance. Silky smooth, radiant..." This ad points out one of the stereotypes that may help make the Asian woman the model of acceptable exotic sexuality. Like an idealized child, she is described as small, docile, available and never demanding. Her body is as "smooth and silky," as the hairless body of a sexually innocent child.

High fashion, too, often makes use of exotica. *Vogue* magazine is especially fond of setting its white models, dressed in "native inspired" fashions, against such backdrops as the Tunesian Oasis of Nefta. Magazines for working class women, on the other hand, only rarely show such exotic fashions or locales. In part this may reflect the fact that the Hilton International Way of Life is a much more familiar fantasy to *Vogue* readers. And while *Vogue* suggests that, for the wealthy, fashion is artful play, the *Cosmopolitan* reader knows that in the realm of Dress for Success, clothing is serious business.

For working women, the exotic is, at best, an *after hours* image created through cosmetics, perfumes and daring sexual practices—all important elements of the "Sex and the Single Girl" success package. Apparently only those who are beyond any doubt white, Western and wealthy can afford to look Third World.

Ans

*"As a Black woman you are always in a noticeable minority and all eyes
seem to be focused on you"*

Moluccan is my identity but that doesn't mean that I have the idea that
I have to look a certain way. What could I do to let outsiders know that
I am Moluccan short of wearing a *sarong kebaya* and my hair in a bun?
And what would that prove anyway? I could be completely assimi-
lated except for the costume. No, being Moluccan is not just something
external; it's deep inside me and it makes itself felt without any special
effort. My identity can not be reduced to my appearance.

I recently bleached a few strands of my hair reddish brown and the
comments I got! "I never thought that you, as a Black woman, would
dye your hair blonde." Now, in the first place, I never thought of it as
blonde and secondly, it is only a couple of pieces of hair. I did it in a
crazy mood for fun. The reaction irritates me so much I've started to
answer, "yes, I've decided to integrate myself in white society and
thought I'd start with a couple of pieces of white hair."

A few months ago, I was in America and was constantly confronted with the image they had of Holland: blue eyes and blond hair.
People could hardly imagine there were Blacks here and that racism
was a major problem. In this country, as a Black woman you are
always in the minority—a noticeable minority. And all eyes seem to be
focused on you. That means I am constantly aware of the need not to
confirm stereotypes in any way. The first time I stood on a dance floor
in the middle of a room full of white people, I couldn't move. My feet
felt nailed to the floor. "Black women sure can dance..."

I also notice that I choose my clothing with some care not to
appear sexually provocative. As a Black woman you are seen as something of a whore to begin with and I just refuse to play to that
stereotype. This despite the fact that I am personally crazy about
sweaters and shirts with low-cut necklines, lace, spaghetti straps, tiger
prints, bare shoulders. But since I was eleven, I've been aware of how
white men look at Black women—the exotic sex object, flower behind
the ear, always available... Until recently, that has been reason enough
to ban low necklines and the rest from my wardrobe.

I really get sick of hearing white people say things like "you Black
women are all so beautiful," though of course I agree. It is the way it's
said that makes all the difference. All too often it feels like just one more
generalization. Beauty is a funny thing anyway. When I hear the

words "beautiful man" the image of a Black man immediately comes to mind. Immediately. But if I hear "beautiful woman" the image of a white woman surfaces in me sooner than that of a Black. Strange, because I generally do find Black women a lot more beautiful than white.

I suppose it comes from the fact that from childhood on, if you read books, watch television, see movies, beauty is always a white girl with blonde hair and blue eyes. It is something that works its way deep into you.

I always resisted in my own way. As a child, I colored in the faces of the women in all my drawings. And they were always dressed in a *sarong kebaya* with their hair in a bun. Though the first time I turned in such a drawing, I remember thinking the teacher wouldn't accept it. At school it was clear that the Moluccan children were considered dumb; nothing we did was right. There was even a dumb and smart class, and the dumb class was three-quarters Moluccan. The smart class was for white kids.

I never said anything about it, but I thought "I'll show them we aren't stupid." From then on I was at the top of my class. My life as a perfectionist had begun. I knew something was wrong, but I didn't yet have a name for it.

I think my first conscious act of resistance to racism was in secondary school. I bought a pair of red shoes; red because for me it is the color of warmth, but especially because it is a color of struggle and power. On one shoe I sewed an I and on the other a K. IK (ME). I was just thirteen.

To the question why I had those letters on my shoes, I explained that I meant to be me, my own person, and that no one else had the right to tell me what that was. The teachers called me egotistical and stubborn, because I refused to be only what they deemed proper for me. It has never been easy to hold on to a strong sense of myself as a Black woman in such a white society.

When I got out of secondary school, I thought for a while that I might like to attend the art academy. Art is such a big word. What I really wanted to do was to make things, draw things, give visual expression to what was inside me. But that is something so personal and so vulnerable, I knew I couldn't do it in a hostile white structure. To survive, I would have to adapt to their norms. For all those years of study I would have had to try to pass. And I know I am no good a making myself acceptable.

Saniye

"Being different has become a constant feature
of my life"

My father had lived and worked in the Netherlands for fifteen years before the rest of the family left Istanbul to join him here. I was twelve then. My mother just couldn't stand being alone any longer. Three days after we settled here, my mother had a heart attack and died. Nothing made much sense after that.

We immediately had to start learning Dutch; we had no friends and very little money. And, of course, we weren't used to being with my father. He had only been in Turkey for vacations; we really didn't know him very well. All in all, it was a very difficult way to start a life in a new country.

My father was never particularly traditional. He was a modern man from the city. And he liked the Netherlands. After all he had been here for a long time and was used to the people and the place. We weren't. My father insisted we try to fit in.

He was convinced that if we didn't adapt, we would face even greater problems in the future. And, of course, on the one hand, he was right. But on the other, it wasn't always possible. Even if we had been willing to totally assimilate, it wasn't always our choice. We were set apart, seen as different because we were Turkish.

Right away on the first day of school, it was my *difference* that was important. The teacher introduced me to the class as a Turkish girl from Istanbul. Though I thought I had dressed pretty much like the other kids, they somehow managed to look much older. We were only thirteen, but the other girls were all wearing make-up. At school in Turkey, we weren't even allowed to have long nails or have our hair hanging loose over our shoulders. I may have come from a modern city, but things were pretty different here.

On the other hand, I was enough of a city child that my class-mates had trouble matching me to the stereotype they had of Turkish children: "How can you be Turkish? Turkish girls always wear head scarves and pants under their skirts." It was all so strange; I wasn't different like that, but I *was* different.

About that time, I remember buying a new pair of pants. Though I've never paid much attention to fashion, those pants happened to be the kind that everybody was then wearing. So anyway, now I had a pair too and wore them to school. But that didn't mean I suddenly fit in. Instead the teacher made a point of telling the class "Look, boys and girls, Saniye can be fashionable too."

Being different has become a constant feature of my life in both countries. If I were to return to Turkey now, even to the city, I would have problems fitting in. To start with, the Turkish government sees us as guests while we are there just as the Dutch government considers us guests while we are here. It's awful to realize that, even in your own country, you are not completely accepted.

The last time I was on a Turkish plane on my way to Turkey, I found that the cabin crew made very obvious distinctions between those passengers they believed to be guestworkers and the rest of us. Because of my modern clothes and my educated speech, I was approached with respect, whereas the more traditionally dressed woman seated next to me was treated so rudely. I couldn't help but think that that stewardess's own mother might well have looked like the woman in the seat next to me. That she herself might have even looked that way before she moved to the city and got that job. But people in Turkey who have become modern, no longer seem able to accept the traditional. To treat traditional Turks as lesser beings is an attitude that diminishes me as well. There I was, a Turk among Turks and still the divisions were made.

The majority of Turkish people in Holland do come from the countryside and have a very different culture than city people. Those differences have intensified my loneliness; not only has it been difficult to make contact with Dutch people, but it is even hard to feel entirely comfortable with my compatriots.

Many rural Turkish people living outside Turkey become even stricter with their children here than they would have been at home. Tradition becomes everything. They are so terrified that their children are going to become Dutch. But it seeems to me at least as important that a child feels comfortable at home so that she doesn't run away at fourteen or fifteen. I see a lot of those girls, four or five a week. They feel like they have no freedom at all in the family. I often hear complaints like "I'm not even allowed to wear my hair the way I want...I can't wear make-up or to go to the movies. My father still buys all my clothes."

It is part of my job to talk with those girls and their fathers. I am the person who deals with women who leave home, women who have family problems, women who have been battered. Sometimes I think I'm just too young for this work. Here I am, twenty-one years old, and I've already had three bleeding ulcers.

Turkish women in the Netherlands

Photo: Bertien Van Manen

When I ask the men what in god's name they think they are doing, all I hear is fear. They have the idea that they are only in this country temporarily to earn some money, save enough to buy something in Turkey and return home. But meanwhile their children are growing up here, and because they are so terrified that they will become Dutch, they end up torturing them, afraid to give them even the littlest bit of independence. The problem only becomes worse as they realize that it is not only the children who will have trouble readjusting to life in Turkey; on holidays home, the men, too, often find that they no longer fit. So they retreat into the Koran, retreat into the home, hiding away from all those things that frighten them so.

When I visit Turkey now, I feel so white. This awful climate means I never get enough sun and my friends are shocked at how pale I've become. I don't know what I should do. Going back will be so difficult and staying here is so terribly hard.

Rhoda

"Beauty for most young girls has become a key
to success

The Caribbean doesn't have just one image of womanhood but several distinct ones. In fact, in Trinidad and Tobago there are at least three separate images based on our mixed history of African slavery, indentured Indian labor and British colonialism.

The economic and personal independence of African women dates back to right after emancipation. Those women lived in the streets, they fought in the streets, they ate in the streets, they danced in the streets. Indian women, on the other hand, have always been saddled with an ideology of Otherness: the Indian woman is not supposed to be like the loud, sexual, uncontrolled, unmarried African woman. She is docile, she is passive, she comes from the tradition of India. In the family, she knows to recognize the man as the boss. The traditional view was that, unlike the Africans who had their families destroyed by slavery, the Indian woman came from India together with her family. This was used as evidence to explain why Indians— unlike Africans—could progress, could have proper families with proper wives.

In fact, the majority of Indians didn't come in families at all. In the early years, far more men than women came over. And the majority of women who did come were not what you'd call "wife material." They were those who were considered the dregs of society: women running away from unhappy marriages, unmarried pregnant women, women who were temple dancers or prostitutes in the ports, or Brahmin women who were unable to remarry. For many of these women, coming to the Caribbean represented an opportunity for a kind of freedom they previously did not have. All the colonial correspondence is filled with discussions of the Indian Woman Problem.

This history has really been hidden. When Indian women have tried to organize politically they have been told "you can't. Remember you are different. You have a different history and background." For many of these women it has been a real load off their backs, finding out that Indian women have not been traditionally docile, passive creatures.

Along with the supposedly docile Indian and the agressive African woman, there was a competing image of womanhood promoted by the British colonial powers: that of the good British housewife. The colonial church tried to institute the Western European nuclear family by, for the first time, making illegitimacy a stigma and insisting that women should give up their economic base to become dependent on men. In reality though, the economic situation never made that completely possible. Besides, the male breadwinner ideology was a totally foreign idea largely, I think, because of the history of slavery.

Under slavery, the person who was a hero in society was the one who could survive doing the least. So for many men and women, the hero was he who could do as little as possible for the white man. This was always more difficult for women because they had small children to care for, but it remained true for men. In fact, especially in the 1930s, many men were kept by women. For these "sweet men," it was important to be handsome and able to please women sexually.

I think even today, while women may be more economically dependent, there is always this underlying rule: if you are dependent on a man you always save some money for when he leaves you. Because that is a very strong possibility. And even if the man brings in the income, you always try to have your own "vex" money. Vex money is the money you can use to leave when you get vexed or he gets vexed. When you go on a date, and a man behaves badly you just say "I walk with my vex money so you watch it. You can't have anything on me."

Those sorts of things are the remnants of a long history of economic and sexual independence among African women in the Caribbean. But the reality now is different in important ways, of course. Many of the jobs traditionally done by women have changed hands, a change of status reinforced by the rise of Rastafarianism. As a part of that messianic religion, women become subordinate bearers of culture in the struggle for Black manhood.

In the Caribbean, where all women were once known as tantie (aunt), in Rastafarianism they are now known as daughter. There is also a real attempt to control women's sexuality. A recent Jamaican song goes "Soldering is what a young girl wants"—that is, welding her vagina shut. Rastafarian women are to be covered from head to knees and their continuous pregnancies serve to control their mobility and their sexuality. But, of course, for these women pregnancy means producing the Black race to fight for the liberation of Africa. And you must understand that the Rastafarian image of women is a reaction to the thoroughly sexualized image imported from the United States. It is a reaction against Babylon—the whole capitalist use of women as a sexual object. So it is a very complex issue.

Recently, a new twist was added to the image of Caribbean womanhood. In 1978, an old school friend of mine became Miss Trinidad and Tobago and then went on to become the first Black woman to win the title of Miss Universe. It was very important for Black women. Of course, the following year, Miss South Africa won and Miss Trinidad and Tobago handed the crown over to Miss South Africa.

But during her reigning year, Miss Trinidad and Tobago traveled throughout the world, met film stars, became rich and famous. When she returned to Trinidad, it was as a member of high society. Whereas before the prime minister had criticized beauty contests, now all of a sudden they were legitimized. She even received the country's highest award, the Trinity Cross. As we say in Trinidad, every Monday morning now there is a beauty contest. Beauty for most young girls has become a key to success.

I have always been against beauty contests and it didn't help my opinion of them that they finally chose a Black woman for the title. When I think of the areas in which we have to validate ourselves as Black women, beauty is just not one of them. The thing that bothers me the most is this: as long as beauty remains such an important aspect of womanhood, some women will just fail to be women.

This interview has been expanded into a scholarly paper, "Transformation in the Ideology of Women and Women's Labour in the Caribbean" by Rhoda Reddock, University of the West Indies, Trinidad and Tobago.

Tania

Tania
"As I discovered my own power, I lost the longing for blue eyes"

Under South African law, I am officially considered Colored. But so is my light-skinned sister with brown hair and my brother who has kinky hair and skin even blacker than mine. The state determines what color you are. At sixteen, you have to fill out some forms, attach a photograph and send them to a state authority where your race will be decided. Differences in color are noted by official subdivisions. For example, I am a Cape Colored whereas my sister is called Indian Colored. Of course, many people categorized as Colored are of mixed Black and white ancestry. In fact, if you can prove having had a white grandparent or parent and are yourself very light skinned, you can even make an application to be reclassified from Colored to white.

Both Blacks and Coloreds are held in contempt by whites in South Africa, but a Colored gets a better wage and can live in a nicer area. That already makes a significant difference. So of course skin color has been incredibly important. Separating people out according to supposed racial categories like Black, Colored and Asian, and giving each group slightly different rights, has been a way of dividing the Black struggle. There is no advantage for any of us in using those terms.

I have felt so proud lately of the demonstrations in Cape Town. Many of the kids on the streets facing the police are young Coloreds calling themselves Black. If white South Africa chooses to make color an issue, our color is Black. It is a Black, not a Colored and Black, struggle we are fighting.

Becoming politicized really does change how you see color. As a child, I longed to have blue eyes and straight hair. It wasn't just that those things were supposedly beautiful, but they seemed to represent a special kind of life, the life I imagined white people had. People with blue eyes seemed to me free of fear, proud of who they were, comfortable and powerful. Gradually, as I discovered my own power, I lost the longing for the blue eyes. My envy gave way to anger.

Making people look the way you want them to is an important part of the colonial process. By taking away a people's culture and pride in their appearance, you literally change the way they see themselves. When I was a kid, the magazine image of Colored beauty was very Western; straight hair and light skin. But next to that commercial image there has always been a political response. Winnie Mandela, for instance, often appears in public in tribal dress. It is a way of reclaiming history for a people whose roots have been dug out from under them. There is real power to be found in recognizing your own beauty.

Women in South Africa do give a lot of attention to grooming, make-up and beautiful clothes. That's something you really notice. People are well-dressed. Part of it has to do with class. If you come from a poor or working class family, you learn to take pride in being clean and well-dressed. It is part of your survival as a poor person.

I taught primary school for a while. I remember telling the children, "you must look neat, your nails must be clean, clean nose, clean dress, clean shirt." "But teacher, I've only got two shirts." "Then wash one out each afternoon." It is part of your dignity.

You need dignity, because whatever else we had was bulldozed down. You should see the way the Black girls dress in Johannesburg. Now they're dressed to kill. Wanting to be beautiful by dressing up is not only a Western thing. The problem is not the desire to be beautiful, but believing that beauty is a question of blue eyes and straight hair.

Strangely enough, I never saw my own beauty until I moved to Holland. I remember the first time someone here said, "you're beautiful," I actually went to the mirror and looked. When I lived in South Africa, being attractive was not for other Black women, but for men, despite the fact that I was well aware I was a lesbian. My relationship was absolutely hidden, so I had to live a double life. Dressing feminine, dressing to look attractive, was a form of protection. It was a way to make myself look heterosexual. If men found me attractive, I felt safe.

When I moved to Holland and was able to come out as a lesbian, I no longer needed that protection. Finally I could dress in a way I found comfortable to please myself. Now that dressing up isn't a disguise anymore, I've really started to enjoy making myself attractive for my friends, my lover, myself. Now I love it, absolutely love it, when people tell me I am beautiful.

Marieme
"Women are just the make-up for our societies in change"

The issue of the veil in Algeria is a lot more complicated than you might think. Most Algerians are Berbers, and though women are supposed to have something covering their hair, in Berber culture there is no such thing as a veil. Still, if you go to the big cities these days everybody seems to be wearing one. Islamic fundamentalists have recently been responsible for the pressure on women to take up the veil, but the veil is more than a religious symbol. It has historical, political and class significance as well. For instance, when a man is promoted and moves his family from the village to the city, the woman tends to take up the veil as a symbol of city life and of her husband's success. When she returns to her village for a visit, she wears the veil to show her friends that she has moved up on the class ladder.

It has also been used as a symbol of cultural resistance to French colonialism. Before the start of the Algerian fight for independence from France in 1954, the veil was only worn in the cities and not at all in the countryside. Yet the image of the Algerian woman as seen through the French colonialist's eyes was of a woman who had to be freed from the veil.

In May 1958, after Algerie Française supporters in the army brought De Gaulle to power, peasant women were brought to Algiers to demonstrate support for what the French called fraternalization. These women were asked to publically unveil and burn their veils as a symbol of their emancipation through Western culture. The idea was to show the French colonizer liberating Algerian women from our backward traditions.

So of course many young women of my generation—the generation of the liberation struggle—adopted the veil for the first time during the fight for independence. There was a whole ideology attached to it articulated by Frantz Fanon. I now find it all very painful. I mean, he really managed to mystify the veil for a lot of us.

Certainly the French used the veil as a symbol, but it was an extremely simplistic response for us to react by reclaiming the veil as our own. I think it made it more possible to tame the demands of women in favor of other priorities—national liberation, class struggle, tradition.

During the period of colonialism when we were faced with tremendous violence and violation, the most urgent task was to put an end to it. Many different political groups joined together in a common front, but each kept enough autonomy to be able to pursue its own political objectives within the front—except for women. We weren't well enough organized before hand so it was far too easy to confuse us with talk of priorities and involve us in blind support of traditions for the sake of a supposedly classless and genderless nation. Women came to bear the burden of keeping up traditions and guarding the national identity. Finally, it became part of a whole process of pushing women back to the most repressive kinds of traditions.

You always have to look at the idea of tradition in terms of power. What is handed down to women as traditional is rarely in our favor. I don't mean that there aren't aspects of our indigenous culture that we will want to draw from, but even then, it should never be seen as a fixed and sacred thing. Just show me a time when tradition was "pure" and a-historical. Culture is not fixed in the past, unchanging and unchangeable. Tradition is constantly evolving.

So, in talking about the veil, you have to first recognize its complicated and ambiguous history. At one time, ten years ago or so, the veil did provide young Algerian women with the opportunity to do more in the world. If they came from very traditional families, wearing a veil was the only way to be allowed to leave the house and attend secondary school. It was good to be able to send girls to school and to the university, even at that cost.

But there is a price to be paid. And now the veil is clearly less and less progressive. So why should we defend it simply because it has some complicated relationship to tradition? Most of those people currently pushing for the veil in Algeria are religious fundamentalists. They certainly don't see the veil as a means to increase the options for women in the world. No, it is just part of the Islamic tradition.

Those in power are always very selective about the aspects of indigenous culture they wish to preserve as traditional. At the same time that the state argues that it wishes to use tradition to maintain a national identity, it is frantically pursuing modernization through industry and development. Those changes are considered acceptable; everyone agrees that our economy must modernize.

What is not accepted is that the outside image should change. And that image is supposed to be synonymous with identity. But for me, that is only make-up. And women are to be the make-up while men get to live in the real world.

In the summer of 1970, the first and only Pan-African Cultural

Festival took place in Algiers. It included a symposium on African culture. The delegate from Ghana made a speech in which he attacked the idea of "negritude." He noted that while African elites were seeking Western industrial development and economic links to the West, they wanted the lower classes to be in charge of preserving indigenous culture. He said something to the effect of: you want them to be the niggers while you yourselves try to be Westerners. It was an historic event, the first public critique of negritude. I remember being delighted because I thought this can be applied word for word to the situation of women.

We are just the make-up for our societies in change. Whether the state has socialist pretentions, as in Algeria, or is a monarchy like Morocco or is openly Westernized like Tunisia, women are in charge of preserving tradition. And the result is continued subservience.

The women I know who have adopted the veil in recent years are most often true believers in Islam. They are very honest people who fall into the arms of the fundamentalists without understanding that they are falling into the arms of the extreme right. The fundamentalists have money—a tremendous amount of money—and an international organization behind them. And they're important because they are the only ones dealing with the real needs of the people. The left doesn't, nor does the government.

The fundamentalists are the ones who provide basic cereals, who create mosques in every building, who distribute clothing. And the clothes they provide are, naturally, Islamic. For women they are in the Iranian fashion covering the entire body with something like the chador. They can encourage the use of the veil simply by giving clothing away or providing it at a very low cost.

In Algeria we don't have a huge media industry with glossy advertisements. The message of how a woman should look passes through political institutions not through the media. These channels are difficult to locate and describe. It might be an article in the paper, or a speech by an official, on what the Algerian woman should be. And of course it comes through everyday repression telling you what a woman should not be.

When women began wearing mini's (and that was not what you would call a mini; it was a knee length dress) we were beaten in the streets by young, very violent fundamentalists. This also happened when women tried to adopt the maxi fashion. Because fashion of any kind is seen as a way of focusing attention on a woman and that is exactly what is not to be done.

Zdena
"Sometimes you'd get a hold of an old Western magazine and you'd try to look just like that"

I was a child of ten or so in the early 1950s, but I well remember the images of the New Czech Socialist People. They were mainly of men in those days—miners and socialist farmers—strong, muscular men. When there were images of women, they were usually portrayed as peasants with scarves over their heads working on collective farms. Or as mothers—tall Russian types with a baby in arms. Another popular early image was of the Socialist Family, again composed of a strong male worker in blue overalls and cap, a tall muscular woman with a child in her arms and a little boy by her side. Of course, nobody in the street looked like that. Nobody is tall and strong; I mean we are a pretty short and fat people.

During the 1950s, women had to go out and work; there was a tremendous labor shortage. Besides, men couldn't earn enough to support a family on one paycheck. Women were especially needed to fill positions in light industry (like textiles) in order for men to move into heavy industries.

There was an accompanying theory of the family justifying women working outside the home. A whole literature developed eulogizing nursery schools and kindergartens. It was argued that it was medically and psychologically superior for babies to be placed in nurseries when they were three months old, if not sooner.

By the 1960s, the image of women—inside and outside the family—was changing. By this time, the artificial production images (the Socialist People) were pretty subdued as we were working out our true image of ourselves and of socialism. It was a time in Czechoslovakia of struggle with censorship; a time in which more, and more interesting films, plays, cabarets and music were produced.

Yet, at the same time, toward the late 1960s, another element was at work: consumer socialism. Khruschev had just declared that socialist countries could catch up to, and actually surpass, the living standards of the West. As a result, we then had the first advertisements and the first images of woman as consumer. The ads were really very funny, modeled on Western images but created without the right working material or equipment to do it properly.

There wasn't much available for women in terms of fashion and cosmetics at that time. But sometimes you'd see a Brigitte Bardot film or get hold of an old Western magazine and you'd try to look just like that. We used to use black shoe polish as mascara, which meant that any time you got it in your eyes it hurt something horrible. But we still did it.

The style was to have highly teased hair shaped into a sort of bun look. Well, we literally used a dried bun fastened under our hair to keep it up without use of hair spray which we didn't have. Anything to look right.

I'm quite ashamed now of that period, of the lengths to which I would go to be stylish. I think we did it more for ourselves than for men. Though in some ways it is always because of men. I mean even Brigitte Bardot didn't devise her own Look. It was created by the men who created her. But I don't think we imitated her primarily to attract men. I think it was more to feel like you were what society expected a woman to be-to know that you fit the image. And that image was a confusing one.

Not only was alternative culture vying with socialist consumerism and the Western ideal of feminine beauty, there were also changes brought on by economic reforms. In the mid to late 1960s, it was clear that in order to make effective economic reforms, which were clearly necessary, inefficient branches of industry, whole factories, would have to be shut down.

And suddenly with the talk of reforming industry, came a new image of motherhood. We women were told that our children were badly damaged by nurseries, that they should never go to nurseries until they were possibly two or three years old. It was such a calculated reversal of the old theory.

Suddenly motherhood was important and mothering was rewarded. Women were granted a sort of state salary when they had a second child, and were paid to stay at home for two years. Theoretically, their job was guaranteed, though in practice they never got the same job back when they returned.

Ideally, it seemed a good idea that the state acknowledge motherhood and its demands. But it wasn't that. Mostly it was intended simply as a way to get women to stay at home. And a lot of women did, too. After all, women's jobs were in any case very badly paid as they tended to be located in industries offering low salaries.

Now, I suppose a woman must be able to do it all—industry and motherhood. Today the image of the perfect woman is one who is mildly successful, like a teacher or someone in middle management. If you are a director, that pushes you into the heroine category—and of those we need only a very few. So the image is of a mildly successful woman, stuck in the middle ranks, who has two children and who has sweetly and gently persuaded her husband to share in some household reponsibilities.

She has done this without bullying or demanding, but through the art of womanly persuasion and has now convinced him to wash the windows or dry the dishes. A mark of success; she has mastered the beast.

And of course, she is also pretty, though she is not gifted with tremendous beauty—that too belongs to a special category of whom we need only a few. But she knows how to make the most of what she's been given by nature, how to use make-up, how to cut her hair, how to dress. There is your successful woman.

Some of these images as presented on television or in the cinema come from the West. Still, the image that is produced here as well portrays women in very much the same way. The Czech advertising industry has gotten much more sophisticated since its early days. You actually see quite nice ads, all of them Western style, promoting cosmetics, furniture, jewelry, food. The new image that has appeared would be familiar to anyone in the West: a successful woman living in a model family. He is about thirty-three, she is about twenty-eight. They have two children. They are beautifully dressed, have a nice flat with smart furniture. They are saving for a summer house or for their holidays at the Black Sea in Bulgaria. And, of course, they have a washing machine, a color television and the most modern kitchen equipment.

A few years ago, I did a little calculating and figured out that this state-promoted model lifestyle would require two wage earners working for twenty-seven years to attain. And yet the people in the ads are in their thirties.

And the amazing thing is that the model lifestyle is not far from the reality for many people. How? Well, for starters we are back to the dowry. The difference is that both the man's and the woman's parents contribute—a car, a flat, furniture. And the rest comes from moonlighting or bribes or cheating.

Just as in the West, if you can get people to buy the image, they spend most of their day trying to get the goods, not thinking about politics. The whole black market economy is tolerated, and for good reason. You can steal, cheat and bribe but dare say something against management, against the party, engage yourself politically and suddenly you hear, "ah, so you've criticized the Comrade Director. And how is it with those two bags of cement you stole last week?"

That is a Damocles sword hanging over everybody and it is a powerful weapon. But this is slowly changing. Living standards were once quite high, and now they are dropping spectacularly. When one part of that very peculiar social contract fails, when people no longer get the prize for which they sold their souls, they are going to think, "ah, maybe I want my soul back."

3
Dress
As
Success

Appearance talks, making statements about gender, sexuality, ethnicity and class. In a sexually, racially and economically divided society all those visual statements add up to an evaluation of power. Economic power, or class position, is easily suggested by a man's use of the standard business suit. An expensive tailored three-piece suit says authority and privilege quietly but unmistakeably. For a woman to get that kind of attention, she must speak up more loudly. Even dressed in designer everything and costly jewelry her appearance makes a less unambiguous statement than a man's $1,000 suit.

Traditionally, a woman dressed in money has been assumed to be making a statement not about herself, but about a man. Her expensive clothing was thought to signal to the world that her husband or other male provider was so wealthy he could afford a clearly useless luxury in the form of this female. In this Veblenesque* interpretation, the woman herself is relegated to the position of a passive object much like a clothes hanger in someone else's closet. While this may well explain a husband's rationale for paying the bills, conspicuous consumption has a special purpose in a wealthy woman's life, too.

> Spurred by the strength of the dollar, Americans came to Paris in droves. Wads of money in hand, they went through town like tornados..."Look at this belt," a Manhattan socialite said at Ungaro's. "It's only $100." Similarly a blouse was "only $600" while a jacket was "only $1200.."..The wife of a New York real estate tycoon dropped a cool $80,000 at Saint Laurent couture. "My husband is going to be a little annoyed," she said. "Oh well."[1]

* Thorstein Veblen, author of *The Theory of the Leisure Class*, published in 1899.

Not only has consuming been one of the few pursuits open to women of a certain class, but being dressed in money demonstrates to the viewing public that the woman's one all important investment—marriage—has paid off nicely. Woman to woman we know that the marriage contract is far from an agreement between peers. At least being well-dressed serves as the visual equivalent of a large pay check.

Women in the role of wife establish social position second hand. A wealthy husband provides access to power for the woman married to him. But this ascribed power has to be made visible. If he has it, you flaunt it—not merely to reflect well on him, but to protect yourself. Dressed in money, a woman looks like someone not to be trifled with despite her sex. She is clearly protected by someone with the ability to do the job.

Increasingly, though, women are finding a need to indicate *personal* financial authority through their dress. Many more women now are breadwinners than in the past. This change is due in part to the women's movement. However, perhaps even more important than feminism is rising male unemployment and inflation making a woman's paycheck indispensable. Higher divorce rates, too, have helped make female financial independence a necessity.

How a woman should indicate professional power through her appearance is still a subject of debate. But all those voices presuming to advise women on how to put together such an image seem to agree on two fundamental things. First, *looking* "successful" is more than half the battle in actually achieving professional success. And second, success is a formula not to be tinkered with—that is, women may now aspire to professional success but should not attempt to redefine it.

Both these precepts have a particular resonance for women. Haven't we always known that how we look is far more important than what we do or how we do it? And as interlopers in the man-made world of business, we tend toward gratitude if someone even takes the time to explain the rules of the game—we may feel in no position to try to change them. Success in these terms is intensely individual and conformity a useful strategy.

———

The restaurant is decorated in understated tones of off-white, salmon and gray. Muted classical music provides atmosphere. Well-dressed professionals are gathered together to lunch. Sitting among them, I feel just slightly out of place; not glaringly wrong, after all I've done well with the material in my closet.

On average, the men around the room are fifteen years older than the women. If my table is any indication, the men are executives, the women their more junior assistants.

It is all so self-evidently good and right and proper and admirable that I stop trying to convince myself that I want no part of it. Of course I do. These people embody success. Their lives are surely enviable.

As the wine bottles empty, tongues loosen; that is, the men become more talkative, the women even more understanding. Talk turns to family problems, love, mortality. The expensive suits and impressive professional titles apparently do not exempt these people from mundane burdens. In the glow of wine and shared confidences, I am tempted to conclude, "See these professionally successful people only seem to be different from the rest of us. They only *look* special. But really we are all the same."

Then I leave the restaurant and move again through the streets of Thatcher's London. And my reconciliation with success disappears. My luncheon companions really do live in a different world. Their clothes are not only expensive statements of how important they *think* they are; their clothes speak the truth. We have allowed our society to be so divided that some people are Important and others quite visibly superfluous.

———

Statements of class provide a sense of place, of belonging. Wealth is coveted not merely for what it can buy, but also for the access it gives to the "right kind of life." In other words, not only are certain products purchased and certain styles imitated for instrumental purposes—dress *for* success—but the image becomes an end in itself. Dress *is* success.

There is a very particular atmosphere in those places where the upwardly mobile and the already arrived gather. These clubs, resorts, restaurants and bars provide a stage on which to display very beautiful clothing and carefully attended appearance. They offer their patrons the possibility to meet other interesting people. Not that the social interaction is straightforwardly mercenary or even sexual. No one is necessarily trying to get anything from anybody else *except* recognition of membership.

Naturally it is not only the elite who gather to be among their own, to see themselves reflected in each other's appearance. Working class bars, punk clubs, women's centers, gay discos all serve a similar

function. And yet there is an important difference. Power is not the password there, except in the idea of strength in numbers. Elite culture is self-congratulatory—we are here because the doorman recognized us as belonging to the invulnerable.

The carefully composed look of success is not without its fashion competition. New Wave culture and punk style are among the most radical forms of visual dissent. At a very minimum, punk is a statement about consumerism. At least initially, the fashion was put together from handmade or second hand clothing. Jewelry was to be found or created from inexpensive materials like rubber, plastic and cheap metals.

Punk has also been an explicit message on the state of the economy. If there is a possibility of a job interview in the near future, one probably won't choose a fluorescent green hair dye or a mohawk haircut. But when unemployment becomes a predictable long-term condition, little is put at risk by looking outrageous. Radically transforming one's appearance can be an exercise of personal power in a life that feels out of control. While it may not be possible for an individual to change the reality of high unemployment, housing shortages and poverty, it is possible to transform one's body into a visual shout: "No, I do not accept the goodness of your goals and expectations. No, I will not help you feel secure in your choices. Do I look frightening? Do I look angry? Do I look dangerous? Do you still feel safe in thinking that the system works just fine? Think again."

Not surprisingly, it is not the Punk but the young urban professionals—the so-called Yuppies—who have become the darlings of contemporary media. Their aerobic bodies and expensive dress speak confidently of physical and economic health. The image is above all reassuring. The system works just fine if you play by the rules. We accept the goals and the methods and we will be among the winners.

Success as it is known in the contemporary corporate world is dependent on a division between winners and losers, with a built in guarantee that more will fail than will be rewarded. Women have always been the structural losers in the system. To be a woman was to be slotted for the position of support staff, both professionally and personally. The reality remains that even today most women will not become senior executives. In fact, most women will not even marry senior executives. The majority of working women will remain on a parallel job ladder which ends in the position of executive secretary or senior administrative assistant.

As anyone with experience in the business world knows, these are the women who run the show, without whom many organizations would come to a standstill. Yet they will never have the money or the authority to accompany the responsibility.

As long as success remains an individual characteristic, only one name will go on the by-line, while research assistants will have to be satisfied with a thank you in the acknowledgements. Secretaries will continue to receive lunch invitations or roses once a year instead of colleague-to-colleague respect and recognition of their partnership in the business endeavor. And women who do make it to a position of recognized power will have to quickly switch class and gender allegiance. Too close an identification with the secretarial crowd, too much empathy with those who come up on the short end of the unequal division of rewards will only be detrimental to one's own climb toward success.

It is arguably an improvement if women as a group are no longer automatically relegated to subordinate positions. But only those who find Jeane Kirkpatrick and Margaret Thatcher shining examples of feminism will believe that this sort of individual success is the same thing as women's liberation.

In the first issue of *Ms.* magazine, there appeared an excellent satire entitled "I Want a Wife," by Judy Syfers.[2] We could all laugh—albeit bitterly—because we knew it was our fate to be the wives never to enjoy the services of one. I suspect that in the 1980s, a similar article describing the reasons "I Want a Secretary and Maid" would provoke a lot less sisterly laughter.

Do women now intend to accept a vision of success that is based on hierarchy, unequal reward, and a strict division of professional and personal life? If so, we would do well to re-read Syfer's original article—this time for tips on what to look for when we go wife shopping.

Those professionals advising women on how to appear more successful do, of course, have a point. It is useful to know what the rules are if you've decided to run the race. Their strategies probably do give individual women a better shot at corporate success. It is of little consequence to them that this kind of strategy reinforces the competition between women, and strengthens the standards keeping most of us from enjoying the respect and rewards already due for our current labor. This is not a surprising atttitude coming from, for instance, John T. Molloy, author of the best selling *Women's Dress For Success Book*, a wardrobe engineer whose only interest is "scientific research, not opinion."[3]

However, it is disturbing when such a visionless perspective comes from within the women's movement itself. *Ms.* magazine, the largest and most important feminist periodical in the United States, ran an advertisement stating:

> When *Ms.* was first launched, scarcely a decade ago, it was a different world. We led the way and we changed the world. So much that we've changed ourselves. We began as the voice of a movement; we've become the voice of a compelling, pervading force...Our vision has been transformed...*Ms.* stands squarely on the leading edge of change, and our readers are making it happen. They're the innovators, the opinion makers. They're among the best educated, highest paid, most activated women in the world.[4]

The narrow class base implied by the proud description "best educated, highest paid women in the world" is troubling. In fact, *Ms.* does a disservice to its diverse readership through such a caricature. Apparently, the *Ms.* vision *has* been transformed; more radically perhaps than the world it claims to have changed. For most women, many of them loyal *Ms.* readers, the world of today still bears an uncomfortable resemblance to that of a decade ago. It is feminism that seems to have changed.

In the early days of the contemporary women's movement, women created strategies of empowerment that focused on shared experience and collective labor. However, we also longed for the individual perques of authority and prestige. But we were operating in an economic structure that insured that while our efforts might allow some of us to "make it," all of us would not. Western industrial society is based on competition and scarcity; equality not of condition but of opportunity. Taking on male bastions of power like the corporate world and opening them up to women meant collectively breaking down the barriers to women's participation. We worked for and achieved legislation that guaranteed us access. But once we succeeded in opening the door, we stepped through and realized that the stairway to the top was narrow and already crowded.

Still, now that the opportunity was there, failure became evidence of personal inadequacy not a political problem. Nor was class (known in America as one's "background") a political concern—provided one knew how to hide it. An entire literature developed teaching the common woman how to reach uncommon heights by "applying" herself and dressing for the part.

Helen Gurley Brown, editor-in-chief at *Cosmopolitan*, wrote a

comprehensive guide book to success in 1982. *Having it All* is based on
Brown's own experience of rags to riches:

> From a problem-ripe youth spent in...small Ozark mountain
> villages, through seventeen secretarial jobs...to my present job
> at *Cosmo* in New York, I have applied almost daily.[5]

Attitude (applying oneself) is key to Brown's formula for
success: use your feminine guile to your best advantage. Do whatever
must be done to move into the spotlight and up the career ladder.

> Could you come in on Saturday? Could you take anything
> home? Can your boss think of anything that would be helpful
> to him personally...or to the project?...You don't care if it's
> menial, you just want to help!...So un-Women's Lib, you say...
> Bullshit!...God knows you aren't taking work home for them,
> it's for you...Not helping simply means you are dumb...It may
> seem that people are "using you" but actually it's the other
> way around...[6]

Try explaining that to the other women in the office. The
problem is that the "mouseburger" on the move makes everybody else
look bad by doing more than she was contracted to, thereby pushing
up the work pace along with employer expectations. On a production
line, anyone caught acting in that fashion would be quickly tagged a
brownnose. Cozying up to the boss at the expense of fellow workers is
hardly in the best tradition of worker solidarity.

Despite her less than conventional views on sex and the single girl
(she is all for it) and her very real concern for and identification with
young working women, Brown's advice can be reduced to the far from
revolutionary strategy "every woman for herself and no holds barred
in the pursuit of male approval." Men like to feel masculine; help them.
Men like accommodating women; give them what they want.

> To be a pleaser and a charmer is not selling out; it is investing in
> happiness (yours)... If you can make a man (boss, client,
> employee) feel more masculine and confident because of the
> way you look at him when he talks, then do...[7]

Brown is clearly talking about a very individual brand of success.
She takes it as a perennial given that for a woman to get where she
wants to go and to pick up the goodies along the way, she will simply
have to fulfill, or surpass, male expectations of women. This strategy
allows for little in the way of female solidarity. Other women are
competition not colleagues. The bosses are the prizes not the problem.
After all, the objective is to marry the man not to usurp his power.

Brown sees it as simple realism for women to do whatever must be done to make it in a male world on men's terms, including shaping her appearance to fit the current fashion: "It is unthinkable that a woman bent on having it all would want to be fat, or even plump..."[8] Chapters on "Diet," "Exercise," "Your Face and Body" and "Clothes" fulfill one third of the recipe for success.

The idea of transforming one's body to transform one's reality is only the logical extreme of a vision that holds success to be an intensely individual quality. You literally must take yourself into your own hands.

> From decent skinny eating...excercising an hour a day, taking vitamins (sixty a day now), no smoking, no drinking, no caffeine, no drugs and being motivated to stay well, your life can change utterly. Mine did.[9]

Despite the fact that Brown's advice centers on how to apply mind (or attitude) over matter in the pursuit of one's goals, she is entirely realistic about the material obstacles facing her readers. When you are working class (lacking in "good family background"), without professional credentials (no "decent education"), when you aren't even especially pretty or bright, you are indeed facing an uphill battle to attain it all. She acknowledges the hard realities of inequality but, far from advocating confrontation, she suggests circumventing them. Brown knows that women with nothing have to enter through the backdoor, but in her optimistic view, at least we're inside.

Once inside and part way up the corporate ladder, the need to disguise your origins becomes imperative. In order to become executive material, you must look as if you come from executive stock—the upper middle class. Enter John T. Molloy and *Dress for Success:*

> We can increase [a woman's] chances of success in the business world; we can increase her chances of being a top executive; we can make her more attractive to various types of men.[10]

Molloy believes at least as firmly as Brown that a woman's business success lies in her own hands. Failure, too, is a personal not a structural problem: "If you have to tell your boss not to send you for coffee, you must have already told him non-verbally that you were ready to go."[11] He quotes "Two extremely successful women" to back him up on this; these women expressed the belief that "The reason most young women wouldn't succeed was because they didn't look like they wanted to succeed."[12]

Dressed in the proper outfit and sporting the proper attitude, the political problem of sexism can be sidestepped. The trick is learning to *accept* reality, not trying to change it. "It is a stark reality that men dominate the power structure...I am not suggesting that women dress to impress men simply because they are men [but rather because men have power]...It is not sexism; it is realism."[13]

In the chapter entitled "Does Your Background Hurt You," Molloy dismisses class as a political problem as neatly as he does sex. Women who intend to move into "The power ranks of American society" first must "learn the manners and mores of the inner circle. And the inner circle is most emphatically upper middle class."[14] Not to worry; his advice is exceedingly specific:

> My research showed that a woman wearing a black raincoat is definitely not automatically categorized as lower middle class. Raincoats are important for women, but not as important as they are for men...The country-tweed look is very upper middle class and highly recommended... The blazer, by its very nature, is upper middle class; every woman should have at least one... Office sweaters...say lower middle class and loser. Don't wear lower middle class colors such as purple and gold.[15]

Predictably, the colors that test best are "gray, medium range blue, beige, deep maroon, deep rust." And the colors to avoid are "most pastels, particularly pink and pale yellow, most shades of green, mustard, bright anything, any shade that would be considered exotic."[16] What we end up with as acceptable colors in the business world are those commonly associated with men and with the white upper class. This look is then defined as "serious." Serious becomes a question of conformity not creative difference, of masculinity not femininity and of the bland over the exotic, i.e. the foreign or racially "deviant."

Racial difference is indeed problematic to success and must be minimized. The process begins with learning to lose any ethnic accent and avoiding exotic fashions. But people of color serious about success are also advised to do whatever possible to transform even their bodies. In African women's magazines, advertisements promote the skin lightner Clere:

> Clere for your own special beauty. We are a successful people and have to look successful. We use Clere for a lighter, smoother skin. Now, Clere will work its magic for you, and make you more beautiful and successful.[17]

Of course, it is not only among dress for success advisors that one finds these prejudices. They just help make them respectable. Even among articulate critics of sexism and racism in contemporary society there is evidence that these standards have been internalized. For example, some feminists collapse gender symbols into the social and political roles with which they have been traditionally associated, and thereby find everything "feminine" suspect, dangerous (reinforcing powerlessness) or at very least unserious: "Serious women have a difficult time with clothing...because feminine clothes are not designed to project a serious demeanor" claims Susan Brownmiller in a recent book on femininity.[18] This begs the question: Is masculine attire really more serious or do we believe it to be more serious because it is male and men are serious, women frivolous?

Molloy's blacklist might overlap in interesting ways with Brownmiller's. "Businesswomen" warns Molloy, "cannot get away with wearing feminine prints...although most of those prints are perfectly acceptable to wear socially they will make men think that a businesswoman wearing them to work is frilly and ineffective."[19] What makes a woman seem ineffective in a work setting may be just the thing for a social occasion when femininity is an asset not a liability. Towards the end of his book, Molloy includes a section on "Dressing to Attract Men" including the "competent look, the feminine look, the athletic look, the slightly exotic look..."

It is as if, after having given advice on how to tone down one's appearance to remove any reminder of gender, sexuality or race, Molloy, too, feels the need to reassure his readers that they can "have it all." It is simply a question of efficient organization of one's closet. Any woman can and should have a rigidly split personality.

The shift from full-time homemaking to double duty (working both for wages and in the home) has helped create a need for new symbols of identity. Women are discovering that they are expected to have not one, but several conflicting images: the wholesome mother, the coolly professional businesswoman and the sexy mistress. No wonder women turn to the magic of wardrobe and make up to provide inspiration for their multiple selves: "Springfever by Elizabeth Arden... New make-up. New inspiration." "I can bring home the bacon, fry it up in a pan and never let you forget you're a man...En Jolie" "Colors that inspire... Let L'erin do the talking." You almost can hear the poor woman sigh "gladly."

The cosmetics industry has been carefully studying how best to make use of this bewildering set of demands made upon working women. Women's wages have been a mixed blessing for the beauty trade. In 1983, *Advertising Age*, an industry trade journal, noted with some alarm an increase in the number of women working outside the home:

> Today, 49% of America's mothers with children under six years old are employed as opposed to only 18% in 1960.... Where women in this group once spent middays at the department store, they are now in the office....Women who formerly had the time to sample and listen and spend money are no longer shoppers. Even when they do visit the store, they do so as buyers.

The subtle distinction between "shopping" and "buying," *Advertising Age* points out, is that the former implies leisure. This distinction seems to be borne out by figures on grocery store cosmetic sales (cheap and fast). In the U.S., they increased by 35 percent from 1980 to 1982.[20]

Without the leisure to linger and shop, a woman may buy what is handy and in the process discover that what she is buying for convenience is not substantially different than the more expensive brand she used to carefully seek out. *Advertising Age* warns: "This is a dangerous conclusion for the industry."[21]

And indeed after decades of constant growth, the beauty trade is now faced with a leveling off of sales and, in some cases, even a slight decline. Not all product lines have felt the squeeze, though. "Customers seem to be turning away from medium price products," the vice-president for marketing of one of America's largest cosmetic companies notes. "They are buying better goods or switching to generic, low-price products."[22] Luxury brands like Erno Laszlo (marketed by the Erno Laszlo Institute—otherwise known by the distinctly less glamorous name of its parent company Chesebrough-Ponds) had an unusually good year in 1983.[23]

The Laszlo example is telling. Inexpensive cold cream and high priced beauty "treatment programs" are both produced by branches of the same company under different names. The entire beauty industry is controlled by a small handful of very large corporations. By the 1970s, twenty-five corporations controlled over 80 percent of all industry profits, and concentration has increased since then.[24]

Often the expensive and cheap products are not only produced by different divisions of the same conglomerate, but they are made of nearly identical ingredients. Even when we know this to be true, we often will buy the more expensive item because the fantasy it offers is more attractive. Psychologist Erika Freeman explains,

An item that promises a fantasy by definition must be priced
fantastically...If a cream begins to sell at 50 cents it will not sell
as well nor will it be considered as miraculous as a cream that
sells for $30.[25]

Even cosmetics purchased for function (to cover skin imperfections, for example) cannot be marketed exclusively on the basis of
quality and good value. In 1980, Hanes launched a new cosmetic line,
L'erin, focusing on its practicality with the "put your face on and
forget it" advertising slogan. It was a dismal failure. A company
spokesman later admitted "We quickly realized we wanted more
glamour in our campaign. We now try to present a glamorous image
for our market in our price range. Actually there are few brands that
have a distinct difference—it's really based on image."[26]

If L'erin was meant to suggest attainable glamour, Yves St.
Laurent cashes in on the unattainable—if you don't already have it,
don't bother. This kind of sales approach is linked to limited
distribution—"exclusively available in select stores"—and profuse
personal attention at the point of purchase—to the right kind of
customer, of course. "The professional make-up artists teach customers the defined method of application to achieve what is referred to
as the Yves St. Laurent Look."[27]

The contrast in marketing between L'erin and Yves St. Laurent
reflects an important strategy in the industry: positioning or targeting
a product for a particular market. The Revlon skin care line is an
excellent example of product targeting: a company executive called
Ultima II the company's "Cadillac Line," Natural Wonder its
"Chevrolet Line" for younger women, and Moon Drops the "General
Motors Line" for mothers and working women.[28]

Naturally, the industry wants you to treat yourself to the best,
and convincing you to buy better is not cheap. It has been estimated
that it now costs the major cosmetics firms at least $5 million to launch
a new product.[29] In one extreme case, Oil of Olay, the company paid
out $20 million for advertising to bring in $50 million in sales in 1977.[30]

Cosmetics, soap and drug industries spend proportionately more
on advertising than any other major industry group. In general, it is
estimated that from 6 percent to 20 percent of company sales must go
to offset advertising expenses.[31] Yet despite the enormous advertising
budgets of the beauty industry giants (in 1983, Revlon Inc., for
example, spent $232 million on advertising; up $31 million over the
year before[32]) cosmetic industry leaders still earn high returns on their
investments. This kind of profit is made possible by producing cheap

and selling dear. Only seven cents of every consumer dollar spent on cosmetics goes for ingredients.

Why do women buy costly beauty products that demonstrably have little purpose other than participation in a fantasy? The purchase of a new cosmetic, the decision to change the color or style of one's hair, the start of a new diet are the female equivalent of buying a lottery ticket. Maybe *you* will be the one whose life is transformed. Despite daily experience to the contrary, we continue to hope that maybe this time, maybe this product, will make a difference in our lives. And if it doesn't, it is still a relatively inexpensive way to visit the mysterious orient of Shiseido, the elite circle of Chanel, the smouldering, sensuous world of Dior. Everything that is so difficult to attain in real life is promised for the price of a new perfume or eye shadow.

I walk into a boutique, disco music urging me to "come on in you sexy thing." Energy is high; everyone but me seems young enough to still believe the buy it, be it promise. The clothes are carefully arranged according to size, color and design. These are the sizes, these are the colors and these are the styles. Which one do you fit? The men and women working in sales reinforce this sense of conformity. They are uniformly young, thin, attractive and suited to the current fashion. They are indeed effective models for the product and a reminder of how I should look.

The promise is that the distance between them (blow dried and sleek) and me (damp hair plastered against my head, nose red from the cold glowing over my inappropriate moustache) can be closed through the magic of making the right purchase. Is it their doubt or only my own that I see reflected back at me in the full length mirrors under the flourescent lighting?

I feel as if I am stripped of protective layers in admitting that I desire to look more fashionable, more attractive. I give away secrets; yes, it does matter to me how I look. I don't trust these pretty boys and girls with the knowledge. Don't use it against me.

I recover later in the variety and jumble of the secondhand shops. They are organized a bit more like I am; the rough edges show, the material is of good quality but it no longer takes itself quite so seriously. Treasures must be hunted for among the junk; and junk was once Product.

Women of all classes know that beauty matters. We don't need Helen Gurley Brown or John T. Molloy or even Revlon to remind us that beauty is magic offering a first class journey through life for the second sex. We are constantly assured that beauty will transform men into admirers and drab reality into romantic gestures.

> ...a man, looking sideways as he talked to his companion, pulled open the door and was about to go through it when he saw her. At once he stepped back, took his cigar out of his mouth and held the door open wide. She passed between the two of them...and there they remained for several seconds, their eyes following her...One of them, carrying for some reason, a dark-red carnation, detached himself and spoke to me..."Mister, pardon me, your beautiful lady has no flower, sir. Please you are allowing me to give her this one.[33]"

The pursuit of beauty is also one of the few avenues to success over which a woman has some measure of personal control. You can mold your body much more easily than you can force access to the old-boy networks or get the job you want, the promotion you deserve, the salary you need, the recognition you are owed. And implicit in the effort is the belief that after beauty follows the job, the money, the love. Having it all... In *Scruples* Judith Krantz tells the story of Billy who transforms herself from a poor, tall, fat girl to a thin beauty and thereby catches the eye—and the $250 million dollar fortune—of her boss:

> By senior year she had reached her full height of five feet ten inches and weighed two hundred and eighteen pounds...it was incredible, a disgrace...[then came] the successful transformation from a fat girl to a thin one...she became her own love object...Many rituals, all concerned with her body took her over...She was thin and she was beautiful, Billy told herself fiercely. Those were the important things. The necessary things. The rest she would have to get for herself...This new Billy could marry anyone she liked. No need for her to go to Katie Gibbs to study to become a dreary secretary.[34]

Personal experience confirms the impression culture gives. The beautiful woman enjoys a measure of respect and attention not generally bestowed on women in a misogynist culture.[35] The beauty industry trades on this reality and the fantasy of escape. Believe in Magic urges the ad for Magie Noire Parfums. Oh, we want to believe. It is one of the ways we hold on despite the disappointments, and one of the pleasures we allow ourselves. The purchase of a $5 tube of lipstick offers a world where women are valued and men pay homage.

How would you feel about having lunch in New York City and dinner in, say, Seattle? About being kissed over North Dakota? Don't answer until you've seen Ultima's Coast-to-Coast colors. Adventurous...

When things get rough, women tend to be a little depressed... it's nice to go and get some cosmetics and feel good. Every single product in the Revlon line stems from a deep seated "need" and the products are all necessary luxuries."[35]

Being a hairdresser is being in the business of making people happy. People come into your salon to look better and to feel better...What we want to sell are happy people. We want to make those women visiting your salon feel like women, feel excited, feel exciting, when they walk out. Because if we can make them feel excited and exciting, they are going to walk out with a smile and bring us more clients. And we'll take all the people we can get...[36]

Fran

"I don't like the way I look right now but I don't judge myself against my models"

We are one of the largest and most prestigious modeling agencies in New York. There are only three or four up there in our class in terms of quality of models, staff and performance—world wide. We interview for new models every morning; on any given day, you come in here and you will see fifty to a hundred potentials wanting to be stars. To pick out a winner that is absolutely gorgeous is easy to do. Anybody could walk into the front office and do that.

To pick out someone who has a quality that only you can see is more of a challenge. I have five or six people doing interviews because each of us has a different eye. Some models have certain imperfections that turn out to be really beautiful when photographed.

We can send a girl we think of as the little girl next door type to a photographer who will dress her up, bob her hair and create someone completely different. Like they say, "beauty is in the eye of the beholder..." or the photographer...or the stylist...or the make-up person. Those people can completely change a person's look. We have a book with four or five pictures of each of our models; a composite of photos that she thinks can sell her. A good model is one who will look different in each picture.

We used to represent girls from eighteen to twenty-eight. Now it starts as young as twelve or thirteen, though we don't like to take them that young. The average age is in the twenties; that is the peak. But if a model can go into different stages in her career, she can go from the *Seventeen* look into *Glamour/Mademoiselle* and then into *Vogue/Harper's Bazaar*. Later, maybe she can become a spokeswoman type and do television commercials. Timing is very important in this business. If you rush a girl and do everything between the ages of seventeen and nineteen, you have nothing to do from nineteen to twenty-nine.

After thirty? Well, a lot of them get married or go into related business. But that is why the money is so big. They can't do this for their whole life. It is short-lived. Models have to earn in ten years what other people can take forty to earn.

It is a very glamorous business, but it is also a very difficult one. The models are selling themselves. They wake up in the morning with a little zit on their face and they panic. They break a nail and they panic. The ones that go out dancing all night pay for it. Their pictures show the rings under their eyes. And then we have to call them in and spank them a little.

There are tremendous insecurities for people who are selling their bodies, their faces. I was a psychology major in college and I would never have believed that I would come across the stories I do.

Models today don't know what it means to be a model. Seventeen years ago when we opened, a model used to walk around with forty to sixty pounds of gear on her back: a black bra and white bra, three different hair pieces and eye lashes—they used to carry eyelashes by the yard. Now it's just brush your hair and swing your head and wear very, very little make-up. Half the time you have to tell them to bring underwear with them because they don't bring it *or* wear it. Years ago you could look down the street and spot a model. Now you can't.

The women's movement is in part responsible for the change. I was very much involved in the rebellion, making a statement through your looks. But I don't think a woman ever really didn't care what she looked like. I always cared a lot about how I looked.

I wish I looked better than I do now. I'd like to knock off fifty or sixty pounds and be as tall as some of my models, but I know it's just not going to happen. Still, just because I don't like the way I look, don't like me right now 'cause I've never been this heavy, I don't judge myself against my models. I work with these people all day long. They are people with the same kind of problems as me or you. They just happen to be beautiful.

Despite being big, I can't see the Big Beautiful Woman model stuff myself. As a big woman, I would rather look at a picture of a nice slim girl and think "oh, gee, would I love to look like that!" I don't think the market calls for changes on the order of older models or bigger models. Basically, I think every woman likes to look at the pages of *Vogue* and see those gorgeous things.

Of course, I personally like to buy things that I know I look good in, not that look good on the pages. But that doesn't mean I want models who look like I do. You'd have to have designers make four million different styles because every woman looks good in something else. That is why we have to have standards.

Men must be six feet tall, a forty regular suit. There are gorgeous looking men that are 5'9" and wear a 39 regular suit. But the camera will cut off about three inches and put on about ten pounds. So in the pictures he won't look that great. And if you stand him next to a girl that's 5'8", he is going to look really short.

Our girls must be from 5'7" and a half to 5'9". Then you can put them with any height guy. They have to be thin, too, so that the garments lay properly. Sure clothes may not look on you quite the way they look in the picture, but then you just have to know what looks good on you, don't you?

Dolores

*"Once somebody pays $200, they're not going to say 'you know, I really
don't like your body that much' "*

When women talk about beauty, they are often concerned about
being objectified, about being seen as a sex object. Well, I am a
professional sex object and I love my work. One of the things about my
job is that I have had to learn what it is that men really want. They have
their fantasies of what a woman they are paying for is going to look
like. If they are paying somebody, she won't necessarily look like
someone they would be in a personal relationship with. It would be a
plus for me to be more like the beauty stereotype, but it wouldn't work
to have the perfect body and not do grooming things.

In Atlanta, it costs $65 a hand for sculptured nails but it's worth it
to me. It is a business expense. If I have a broken nail it might be what
stands between me and this guy saying "yeah, I want to spend $150 on
you." Men would rather have me have ten great nails, a really quality
make-up job and designer clothes than to be thinner.

When I was a kid, I saw an "I Love Lucy" show where Lucy and
Ethel had mistaken this guest star at Ricky's club for a call girl. This
woman is walking around with furs and diamonds and the men think
she is the greatest thing that ever happened, doing everything she asks.
Though this woman is better dressed than Lucy or Ethel ever have
been and has Fred and Ricky under control (something their wives had
been trying unsuccessfully to do for every episode since I'd been alive)
Lucy and Ethel are treating her like dirt. I said to my mother "what's
going on here? Why is Lucy treating her so badly?" And my mother
whispers "they think she is a call girl." She *whispers*. Nobody is there
but us. I said, "I think that is what I want to be when I grow up."

That was my introduction to the idea, though it was a long while
before I did anything about it. First I went to college. I know a lot of
women hook their way through college because it is fast money and
you don't have to put in forty hours. But I didn't have time to take an
hour off to turn a trick. I had to study all the time. After college I got
what were considered good jobs like being an administrator for a radio
station. I wanted to know what it was like to be an executive, to do
work women just didn't get a few years earlier.

It was shit. I did it well enough, but it was really not the kind of
work I enjoy. A couple of women at the radio station also worked as
call girls so I had an easy introduction. The first time I went out on a

job, I knew it was a very important decision I was making. I wasn't desperate for money. I was doing it because a friend from the station had a dentist appointment and had a job lined up. I went as her.

I knew that as soon as money passed from his hand to mine I would be a prostitute forever. Society makes that distinction. I had also heard all this stuff about how horrible and degrading prostitution is, so I was prepared for some kind of degrading experience. But I knew I was tough and would get over it.

I took the money and thought, "okay, this is it"—and nothing happened. Then we had sex and I thought, "okay, this is it." Nothing. So that was what it was like. I didn't feel terrible and I had a lot of money. I was about twenty-seven.

Both my parents were shop owners. As a prostitute you really do own your own body, whether the government says so or not. It's like a self-contained shop. I am not bought or sold. Clients buy a service and to a certain extent a skill. If nothing else, they buy your skill at putting up with their bullshit. You have to be delighted, be into everything that they are, hang onto their every word.

My work has made me more aware of my body. I am constantly dieting. I lean on working as a motivation. If I can't get it together any other way I can just think about how much money it costs me to be overweight. And I am careful about my skin. I don't exactly fear getting older, but I hate seeing my body deteriorate. I can see the wrinkles slowly forming. For me this is dramatic because I want to keep working. In Europe, women work until they are about sixty. But in the States, it is hard to work past your mid-forties. All I have is ten or fifteen years left.

Once I realized that my longevity in the business depended on my being able to look good, I started to do research into which products really work. The woman who originally taught me how to work was in her late forties and she looked great. She taught me a lot of stuff about taking care of my skin, what chemicals I did and did not want to use on my body, what really worked and didn't.

It costs me about $300 a year just for these face creams. But to really prevent wrinkles, you've got to stay out of the sun. Don't move your face and don't touch it. Don't make any really big expressions with your face. I have a list of cosmetics that really work: which lipstick does in fact stay on for four hours. I figured it was something I had to learn. A trade skill.

I haven't always been so careful. Until I was about twenty-two, I had pretty much used being attractive to men to get what I wanted. And then I consciously rejected it for a number of years. I wore ugly clothes, ate what I wanted and gained a lot of weight. It seemed a good vehicle to get over the feeling that I had earned my whole life off my body.

Now I feel like I'm over that. I've proved to myself that I can do intellectual work, can hold a "man's" job and can be valued for other than my body. Now I'm just glad I can get on with doing what I really like. Generally I love my job, and I like the fact I am getting paid so well to do it. It isn't just the money, but the money is a symbol in our society that what you are doing is okay. Not only okay, the more money you make, the more okay it is.

When I get back to New York next week, I am supposed to see a man for the first time for free who started out as a client. He is a great lay and a really nice guy—somebody who, had I met him under different circumstances, I would have probably gone out with anyway. And I am terrified.

I don't like the idea of going to bed with someone without them paying me. It's tied up with a feeling of worth. When I'm being paid, I have a tremendous amount of power over the situation. Now that I've agreed to see him for free, I feel like I am relinquishing that power. I feel very vulnerable.

And I am very concerned about my body. If they are paying me, I feel like they've made this decision that they like my body. When they fork over the money, I know not only have they decided they *want* to like my body, they are *going to* like it. Once somebody pays $200 ($50 for my agent and $150 for me), they're not going to say "you know, I really don't like your body that much." But somebody who is getting it for free might be more critical.

Lisa

"When a client comes into my shop, I say 'okay, so talk to me. What does this hair have to do for you?' "

One of the reasons I decided to be a hairdresser was because of what was happening around the issues of beauty and identity in the early 1970s. It was an issue not just for women but among leftist men too—men who had had ponytails but were now going bald, or who wanted to drop the 60s look without turning into GI Joe.

The issue was a devastating one for my women's community in 1972. The real grassroots working class women who were very political were also very invested in their teased up, dyed and bleached hair and Maybeline Look. Alliances were just starting to happen between the new activists—such as myself—and these women. We were both fighting for day care, better medical and dental coverage, that sort of thing. My own women's group was in crisis about issues like whether you should shave your legs and underarms, whether to wear make-up and make yourself look good.

They didn't know what to do with the beehive style these other women hung onto. My feeling was that women should be able to do their hair and dress up as much as they needed to feel their own power. And if those women wore beehives and felt more powerful inside the system they had to deal with, then why should we make it an issue?

I had gone through a period myself of no make-up and an Afro. But when I then had to float inside the political system, it worked against me to have black hair on my legs and to neglect the way I looked. It is inherent in this culture that if you are appealing and attractive you get further. Period. That is simply the case. Our women's group disintegrated around these issues.

Beauty school attracted me for a lot of idealistic reasons. There wasn't anybody relating to beauty in an upfront fashion in the women's movement and it *was* a problem. It was clearly a problem. All of us wanted to look good and not many of us had skills on our own to do it. I realized at that point that there wasn't anybody out there who could relate to me or my friends.

I also discovered that the field of cosmetology had really established itself in the Depression. And since it seemed the economy was going to get worse, maybe beauty school would offer security in a trade. It was quite a blow to my family that I decided to become a hairdresser. They saw it as a gum-chewing, bubble-headed trade. A real lower class thing.

Beauty school was a culture shock. The first school I attended was run by an old patriarch. Almost all the girls were right out of high school, coming from very poor families. They were stuck in a dormitory above the beauty school, basically going from their parents and high school to this older man.

He made them feel cheap in a lot of subtle ways. Beauty schools are a business and they are an enormous rip off for the student. You pay a fair amount of money and although you learn a trade, you are there working on a clientele that pays the school for your services.

I tried three or four schools; they were so awful I kept looking for a better one. I really felt like I was in the belly of sexism and racism all at once. Going through beauty school was definitely more rugged than the anti-war movement. I was twenty-seven when I started—older than the other students. Because of my age and because I was confrontational, I got thrown out a lot. I demanded, for instance, to learn haircutting. Most of the time they try and get you to do a lot of shampoo-sets.

Beauty schools still teach a look that has to do with the 1950s—the Jackie Kennedy Look. You can't get that with normal, healthy hair. You have to have it permed or colored or something so you can set it and have it hold a tease. People teaching in beauty schools are still invested in the look and for good reason. They believe you want to do stuff to hair that will bring people back *regularly*. Hair cuts just don't have to happen regularly. And let me tell you, I've learned that. I really have to put out in terms of clientele for just hair cuts because your talking about people coming back every two or three months instead of every other week.

There is a real difference here between Black and white shops. In Black shops, customers do tend to come back every other week. You wash, dry, straighten, press and then curl the hair—a three hour process in all.

The people in this business who promote natural hair care as opposed to the teased and set or straightened and curled look are more often than not people who are professionally ambitious. The elite school of hair cutting started with Vidal Sasson in the 1960s. He moved away from the artifical sprayed, teased, bubble, ratty number to natural hair you "could run your hands through..." A lot of his promotion was based on sex appeal but he elevated the class trip for hair dressers.

There was a split in the cosmetology field between the natural hair folks and those who continued to promote the old fashioned story of

"Sure you can dye your hair, sure you can bleach it, sure you can press it, sure you can perm it. Hey, nothing wrong with that." In a sense they were saying, "listen this is how the industry made it. This is what you need for your business to generate work."

The market today has been glutted with hairdressers so the look in hair is getting much more into coloring, teasing (oh yes, they are even teasing hair again, but now its called french lacing), perming, and doing short hair cuts (because they have to be maintained, right?) The industry will never be truthful about why this has shifted; it will be blamed on one thing or another. But it is really because we need the business.

And maybe that's not an entirely bad thing. Those of us in the business may be able to make enough money to survive at least at a maintenance level. During the Depression, beauticians did survive longer than most, because if people can't afford to go to Europe, they can still afford to treat themselves to a good hair cut.

I think it is riskier what we do now than what used to be done. Clients used to almost expect that you were going to ruin their hair. Now you've got to color and perm the shit out of it, and their hair still has to feel great and natural and not like acrylic.

But in the long run, I am really glad I am where I am today. The initial reasons why I started in this trade have come full circle. Years ago, I met a carpenter dyke in overalls and fuzzy funky. She recently decided to get a straight job. She didn't know how to dress, she didn't know how she should wear her hair. I had the chance to help her explore all that stuff. Which is, after all, why I chose this field.

I was with a woman the other day who is striking but her hair is so unsightly. It came right out of my mouth: "Vern, why does your hair look so awful?" She basically said "If I feel this bad inside, I have to look this awful." My mouth dropped: "You don't. Not in the 1980s, you don't!"

It is really tricky working on people. It is candid, it is intimate, it is brief. And it is so personal. I feel like I have to be pretty clear and forthright about what I see.

A majority of my clients will come in and say "I need a shampoo, cut and somebody to talk to for an hour." At some level we are grossly underpaid. There is no way I am going to be adequately compensated in a monetary way for what I do. It has been a real struggle for me, as a woman, to not give myself away every hour, every day.

I underestimated this job enormously, the emotional and physical stress and fatigue. People in my field burn out. That is why there is

Leonie

such a turnover. Drugs and alcohol are rampant. We discovered a few years back that EST (Erhardt Sensitivity Training) was making a big push into beauty shops as a recruiting ground. There were whole shops that were EST. People who go through beauty school are never given any real preparation for the kind of information exchanged during work. It is understandable they might find EST appealing; something that gives people a dialogue that sounds genuine and close but is far away.

When a client comes into my shop, I sit her down and say "okay, so talk to me. What does this hair have to do for you?" I am into helping people play with make-up, play with hair. I don't believe in putting on make-up to just make yourself look "pretty"—which is what most of us are taught. I think we should use make-up to bring out a strange feature as opposed to trying to hide it.

One function of make-up tends to be to neutralize. That is something I had to confront with make-up because I already felt neutralized enough. With a little bit of make-up, I can look like a cupcake airline hostess. I didn't want that. For me, make-up has been a way to try to look different, more interesting.

A lot more women seem to be experimenting with their appearance these days. It is certainly now the minority of women who come in and say "my husband wants me to have long hair." But they are there and I just have to respect that. I try not to step out of bounds by saying "but that is absurd!" Actually, the majority of my clients are interested in exploring who they are. They don't usually say that they are interested in appealing to men, but sometimes women do say "I want to look sexy." I think that's great. If you decide you want to look sexy and you have some control over creating that look, terrific.

I had a woman come in the other day who said "give me a 'fuck me' hairdo. I am just dying; I haven't been with anybody in ages!" So we did. We cut and colored her hair and it was great. She looked fantastic. But by the time she got home, she called and said "I can't do it. I can't go from being a wallflower to this. It is too intense!" It was tasteful, but it was definitely "fuck me." So we had her come back and we toned it down a little.

Projecting an image is always a problem for women. It's not easy, for instance, to find a comfortable professional look; a look for women that doesn't deny some hint of sexuality period, whatever the preference, and a look that still gets them taken seriously. Men wear suits and ties everyday as a sign that they take themselves and each other

Diana

*"There is a fantasy aspect in life that joining
dress for success serves to deny"*

A friend of mine had his tailor make me a gray corporate suit for my fortieth birthday. I've only worn it once as a suit, but I do like to wear the jacket often. I mean this is a totally corporate jacket; it reeks of the conservative corporate world. I make a joke by wearing it with sweat pants. I wore it as a suit just that once on a job interview after graduating from professional school. It was a disaster.

I felt bad tempered—like somehow I'd been done in. Like I was accepting something I ordinarily wouldn't have accepted. I didn't feel at home in myself. I was trying to pretend that I would accept corporate rules when the fact is, I won't.

Many women dress in corporate uniforms in an attempt to be taken more seriously. But we can't really do much more than remain a token. And being a token imposes a whole set of rules about behavior, the first and foremost of which is not to threaten the power structure.

Wearing a dark blue suit simply states that you accept the values of corporate culture. It is not going to get you anywhere, though it may protect you from some kind of punishment. You prove by your dress that you have loyalty to, and accept the goodness of, corporate life. And that you very much wish to be a part of it. That is not in any way an exercise of free choice. You have to dress that way just to walk in the door. But that is not the end of the process.

Testing goes on at every level; after the uniform, will you also stand for off-color humor? will you accept stories of sexual conquest? will you join in on racist jokes? The ante keeps on going up and up and up. The point of the test is that a true token never threatens or deviates from the norms of the dominant culture.

And as a token, you are made to understand that you are the exception. The woman or person of color must then guard the gates against upcoming women or other people of color. You are there on the basis that you are exceptional. So wearing that suit gives you access—it's simply a card you must have to get through the door—but it doesn't get·you anything positive.

It has been my experience that the point of getting everybody into certain kinds of outfits is that they are then instantly placeable. The dress for success uniform is promoted as desirable on the assumption that everyone wants to look rich, suave, upwardly mobile. Any execu-

tive, male or female, can tell you the price of a suit to the last dollar just
by looking at it. It is fantastically easy to determine that that person
makes $50 a week and that person makes $1000 a week by their suit.

There is a disturbing lack of individuality here. People have
bought very beautiful clothes, but they don't make them their own.
They don't say "how could I wear this gray suit and make it special,
make it mine." They say "I am going to wear this gray suit because it
shows very clearly to anybody with a trained eye that it cost $600,
$1000, $5000."

The whole business places most people forever in the "I'm trying
to rise" category. Then those people with real power can just stomp on
them. It makes it very, very easy to control people by placing them
according to class. I think that is the most important function of those
uniforms; to place people and hence to control them.

My basic principle of dressing is that I refuse to be identified by
my appearance. It is a way of saying that I will not accept my place, my
role, my slot. I am not a corporate banker, I am not a hippy. Yes, I make
breakfast, yes I clean my toilet, yes I go on holiday and yes I buy and
wear rhinestones. Yes I do intellectual work, yes I do mothering work,
yes I do social work. But I do not accept that you should look at me and
say "ah, there is a social worker;" "ah, there is a mother;" "ah, there is a
corporate person;" "ah, there is a member of the upper class."

This is certainly easier for me than for some. There is obviously a
huge financial aspect to dressing. I come from money, and though the
reality has changed, the spirit is still there. Though I may no longer be
rich, deep down I know that I will never really have to worry about
where my next meal will come from. My life has been downward
mobility, or sideways mobility. But a different direction, anyway.
I've never had the Fitzgeraldian desire to move up. So my clothes
never have had to make that kind of upwardly mobile statement. I am
sure that some people can achieve that independence without having
had money. I mean there are stronger characters than I, let's face it. But
having had money gave me a real boost.

Still, class isn't everything. I never would have dressed the way I
do now when I was younger. Never, never, never. When I went to
school, to college, when I worked in Washington, I wore class and
gender appropriate little silk dresses.

I didn't really change from all that until my forties. There was a
big change in my life when I left my husband and lost my money—
it concentrates the mind wonderfully. Playing with clothes was a way
of rebuilding my life from the outside in. Experimenting with clothes

and with life, it all sort of went together.

There was a six or eight year process where things changed dramatically in almost every aspect of my life: my sense of how life should be lived; of how we should connect with each other; my values; everything. And how I dressed was a part of all that—a reflection and a symbol of the changes. It was also a change that gave immediate gratification.

I think there is also a real function of age at work in the way I now dress. Women get politicized as they grow older. Younger women are treated more equally than they ever will be again in their lives. One of the radicalizing experiences for a woman is to get married and discover it is not an equal partnership. You have children and find out who is expected to take time off from work when necessary. You grow older and see who gets attention and who doesn't. These life experiences can make us increasingly disabused of any illusions that we may have had about equality.

That absolutely was my experience. And I think part of the way I dress is to say I want to take my history with me. I have not chosen to have my identity through a man or through one single profession. I really have come to believe that we, all of us, can be revolutionaries and artists; intellectuals and writers; dreamers and housewives and mothers. And wish our children to have a hot breakfast and neatly braided hair, and a bunch of flowers on the table. Because it is nice to be in a beautiful environment and have things that are fresh and coffee that is hot. Good things. And all of that is in each of us.

Our effort ought to be to use as much of us as we have; to use the pallet of our gifts, feelings , experiences. One way to do this, for me, is through clothes. The idea is to cut through peoples' stereotypes: "Oh, I know what that person is...she's a working woman" so then you treat her one way; or "oh, that person is a housewife," so you treat her another way.

Clothes, sometimes just by confusing or startling people for a minute, can give you the chance to be seen afresh. I also just plain think it's fun. There is a fantasy aspect in life, something that joining dress for success serves to deny. Why should we save our silver shoes for after hours? I mean, how many of us go off to galas anyway? Part of me says it is disgusting to go to galas. That doesn't mean it is disgusting to wear silver shoes. Dorothy wore silver shoes and she had a pretty interesting adventure.

Now when I go to my closet, I have only one rule: try never to put the same things together twice in quite the same way; keep things turned upside down so that I don't get settled into being one thing, one person, one idea. I like to dress in a way that is personal and artistic but that also has a kind of joke in it. I wear silver or gold dancer's character shoes almost every day. I like being in the tradition of dancers. The shoes are sturdy and cheap. And they are funny.

I don't mean to suggest that I want the way *I* dress to be taken as a rule: why doesn't everybody take clothes from the thrift shop the way I do and make them into funny costumes? I don't think it should ever be a "should." But I do think we could enjoy ourselves more by dressing in ways that help keep our spirits up. To me it is all part of doing the work to be done without letting them get us down.

Joolz

"Punks are rejecting their class position but you have to be there before you can reject it"

I was nineteen when I married a man who became a Satan's Slave. During the time I was with him, I looked pretty normal. Bikers don't like outrageous looking girls—at all. They do like "nice-looking" girls, though. And they prefer it if you have long hair. It fits with the heavy metal image.

You aren't to wear too much make-up or anything like that, and you wear jeans or trousers because you are on the bike so much. Though some of the girls did wear miniskirts which I always thought pretty stupid under the circumstances. The men clearly liked very girly girls. Oh, and they preferred blondes!

I never paid too terribly much attention to how I was supposed to look. I wore my hair short. It was more comfortable under the helmet. And I used to walk around in boy's clothes all the time. It was a bit of a problem for my husband in the club. But eventually they accepted me because they decided I was artistic and if I was an artist I was allowed to be eccentric. In general, the women were expected to be very domestic and they were.

The club is a close tribal community. Because my background had been so insecure, I found it very reassuring in the beginning. But after five years, I left. It had become too restrictive.

Even before I left my husband, I already had become interested in the punk image. I had already dyed my hair pink—something which didn't go down well in the club.

To dye your hair this color, you've got to first bleach it absolutely white, to strip it right down to the roots. I've had it this way for four years now. Pink was an easy first choice; it was a fashionable color, if you remember. Shocking pink and fluorescent green, those were the colors associated with punk. Nowadays, I have it colored a bright scarlet, Fire Red.

Even when I was a child I wanted colored hair. I remember wanting waist-length green hair because there was this puppet in a children's show on television, a mermaid who never spoke but was extremely beautiful and had long green hair.

I've always tended toward fantasy, the fantastic. In fact my image may have more to do with fantasy than punk in the pure sense. Punk started off anti-fashion. So you set out to make yourself look as anti-pretty as possible. But I've always been too insecure to do it properly. I worry too much about what I actually look like.

My mother is very beautiful—feminine, small and pretty in the magazine style. I take after my father who is big. When I was a child, my mother was very disappointed in me and was always trying to make me more presentable. Other people's mothers used to shout at them for wearing make-up; my mother used to shout at me for not wearing any.

When I was an adolescent, I suffered very badly from acne. I was also overweight. So I was sort of a tall, fat, spotty teenager. I had good teeth though. My mother used to tell me "you have good teeth; smile, it's your best feature."

Having been a hideous adolescent, I've always been too insecure to intentionally make myself more hideous. I tend to sort of go to the "glam" side of punk rather than the anarchy end. I always wanted a Mohican, but I never quite had the nerve to shave my head. I did have very, very short hair at one point, and I looked like a dog. And being big as well I was mistaken for a boy all the time. There are lots of things I wish I had the nerve to do with myself, but I just can't.

It's relative, of course. I suppose the way I look appears pretty outrageous to other people. Something like having a pierced nose I don't even think about anymore. But a lot of people seem to find it shocking.

My tattoos draw a lot of attention too. I got tattooed for the first time when I was about nineteen. I had one on my wrist and another around my ankles. I thought they were alright at the time —a sort of bracelet of flowers. But I only recently met a really good tattooist and have had new tattoos done over the old ones. These are in the Celtic style and are much better and much more extensive. Tattoos and tattooing fascinate me.

There are moments, though, when you get tired of it all. Everybody who looks this different feels that ways sometimes, even if they don't admit it. There are mornings when I wake up and know I have to go down to the shops and wish that I looked like a perfectly ordinary person. But they are not often enough for me to want to change anything.

Not too long ago, for a giggle, I borrowed a plain brown wig off a friend and put it on. It looked pretty convincing. I didn't put on much make-up and went to a gig that way. People who have known me for months and months didn't recognize me.

It was tremendous. But after a while, I didn't find it tremendous at

Joolz
Photo: Francesca Sullivan

all. I found it extremely unpleasant. I actually entered a state of panic. I
was so relieved to take the wig off and be myself again. I felt I had lost
my whole personality. My whole statement was gone and I really
hated it.

The tattoos are the big thing actually. The scarlet hair you can just
cut off if you get tired of it. But when you take the step of having big
tattoos so close to the hands, you really make a permanent statement,
especially as a woman.

I always wear long skirts and I always wear black. I don't wear
jeans anymore because I wore them for so long when I was biking that
I just got sick of them. They feel constricting to me. Same with
underwear.

Despite all the black and the tattoos and the skull rings, some of
my stage costumes, made of lycra and sequins, are extremely glam. I
love feather boas and fans. But always with studs; say a studded belt at
the waist. It is the combination that appeals to me. To be too completely glam would be tiresome. I like to confuse the eye.

The most important statement I am making through what I look
like is one of strength. I have a strong personality and want to indicate
that straight away. Especially in the business I am in, it is important to
have a strong image. Not just from the point of selling your records,
but more importantly so that from the moment you walk into a venue
you are noticed by the sound crew, the security men, everyone.
They've got to know right away you are not someone to be messed
with. This is particularly true for a woman. The rock business is
totally sexist. If you are not a strong person, they will walk all over
you.

Of course sometimes the way I look frightens people I have no
reason to want to impress with my strength. I was taking a train
recently that was absolutely full—people were standing in the
corridors—and there was an empty seat next to me but nobody would
sit in it. People will often stare, but they don't want to get too close and
only rarely will they try to make contact.

Sometimes it seems that people feel that if you look "odd" it is a
license for them to abuse you or threaten you; it's as if the normal rules
of politeness in society don't apply anymore. You've given up straight
looks, therefore you've given up any right to be treated with respect.

A lot of people, particularly middle class people, look at punk and
think it is a working class thing. But actually there are few working
class punk rockers. Only children of the middle class can afford to look

ragged. It *is* a class statement, but not in the way people tend to assume. Punks are rejecting their class position, but you have to be there before you can reject it. And I am not saying that rejecting everything that's expected of you is easy.

It is, in fact, very difficult to actually put yourself outside of society; to appear so different that you are beyond the normal relationships most women have. I don't blame girls who are secretaries during the day and backcomb their hair a bit at night to come to the clubs. For those girls, punk is just fashion.

In a way, I am jealous of them because, in the end, they can become normal. They can submerge themselves in the great stream of weddings and tumble dryers. But I also think that, somewhere inside them, they're disappointed. They know they have experienced a failure of nerve.

I have my hair done by a woman named Lorraine. She works in a very small salon in the suburbs. Every time I go in there, I see this row of ladies with The Perm under the dryers just having had The Cut—which ever one it is at the time. I once asked Lorraine "don't you ever get tremendously sick of doing this?" And she said "If another woman comes in who wants that Perm I'll scream and go mad!" But of course she'd then go and start rolling up the next woman's hair...

The clients watch her working on me and they are fascinated. They'll come over and feel my hair and ask questions. It must be tremendously tempting for them to say "the hell with it; make mine scarlet too!"

4
Ugly
As
Sin

Social expectations create a looking glass into which we are invited to gaze while establishing a sexual identity. A woman standing before this mirror will find her image framed by the presumption "female is woman is feminine is heterosexual." Against the warped surface of these expectations, our individual combinations of biological sex (female/male), social sex (woman/man), gender (femininity/masculinity) and sexuality (erotic preferences) cast reflections as seemingly deformed and laughable as the distortions of a fun house mirror. But rather than blame the mirror, most women will attempt painful contortions in an effort to create a more "normal" reflected image.

Few people can effortlessly embody the Real (masculine) Man or the Real (feminine) Woman. Gender is a social construction: that which is considered appropriate to man is masculine, that which is seen as appropriate to woman is feminine. If it were simply a question of biology, there would be no need to talk of "appropriateness"—the categories of masculinity and femininity would collapse into male and female. Masculine would simply be what a man is and a male transvestite like Boy George would be seen as no less masculine than he is male.

Instead gender tends to mean the culturally determined way members of a sex *should* behave and appear, even if it comes no more naturally than plucked eyebrows or a firm handshake. The existence of only two gender packages of behavior, mannerisms, appearance, and emotional responses is a reflection of the fact that there are two sexes.

In heterosexual relationships, a dominant masculine male coupled with a supportive feminine female is generally presumed to be both natural and ideal. But real life points to much less rigid arrangements. Not only do many couples defy categorization according to such closely defined roles, in some relationships the gender roles and sexes are fundamentally reversed.

119

Television situation comedies and newspaper cartoons routinely point up the mixed gender dynamic of the henpecked husband with the overbearing wife, the bewildered little guy entirely dependent on the woman running his life. The competent, assertive woman and the emotionally dependent man are considered a social joke despite the fact that this is a far from uncommon feature in private arrangements.

If such a mixed gender relationship is a strictly *private* arrangement, it is because the fear of effeminacy is at the heart of heterosexual masculine identity. In *Hearts of Men*, Barbara Ehrenreich notes that in the post World War II period, the description of the mature adult American male was of a married heterosexual as homeowner and father and well established on the career ladder. Any man who deviated from this pattern was considered immature and presumed homosexual:

> In psychiatric theory and in popular culture, the image of the irresponsible male blurred into the shadowy figure of the homosexual. Men who failed as breadwinners and husbands were "immature," while homosexuals were, in psychiatric judgement, "aspirants to perpetual adolescence."[1]

An important key to loosening the masculine burdens of the bread-winner/husband role was the new image of the playboy, promoted in the magazine of the same name. *Playboy* promised men that it was not necessary to take on the responsibilities of home, wife and dependents to prove one's manhood. The playboy was single, selfish and still a Real Man. The Playboy Bunny nude centerfold was the symbol of male virility, of the single but straight theme: "The playboy didn't avoid marriage because he was a little bit 'queer,' but, on the contrary, because he was so ebulliently, even compulsively heterosexual."[2]

Homosexuality was not merely a deviant and therefore unacceptable minority sexual preference, it was a gender *identity*. Gay meant Not a Real Man. Even as late as 1969, psychologist Lionel Ovesey confidently wrote of the close relationship between "failed masculinity" and homosexuality:

> ...any adaptive failure—sexual, social or vocational—may be perceived as a failure in the masculine role...This equation is the following: "I am a failure equals I am castrated equals I am not a man equals I am woman equals I am a homosexual."[3]

When the props of masculinity were removed—fatherhood, marriage, head of household, career man—the substance of what it was to be a man was threatened. This came, not coincidentally, hot on the heels of World War II in which women temporarily had assumed jobs traditionally filled by men and hence had broken through parts of the gender barrier. This challenge to what it was to be a woman implied an equal challenge to what it was to be Not a Woman.

It is especially in periods of social reorganization that the fear of a breakdown in the two sex/two gender system is strongly felt. Thus in the early years of the second wave of U.S. feminism (late 1960s and early 1970s) direct challenges to structural limitations on women's full participation in economic and political life were coupled with assurances that feminists were happily heterosexual and looked just like the woman next door.

Lesbians were an embarrassment and a concern, and not merely because the movement feared taking on the additional and controversial issue of sexual preference. More importantly, feminists worried that taking on lesbianism would mean taking gender on board. This would have threatened the civil rights gloss of early feminist demands.

If feminism could present itself as purely a civil rights movement, it had a chance of being seen as acceptable. Women could be identified as a special group, different from but equal to men and deserving of fair treatment in occupational opportunities, wages and an equal number of orgasms. Ironically, the civil rights approach was also popular among certain parts of the gay movement itself. Fierce debates raged, and in some places continue to be fought, over such issues as whether publically and blatantly defying the masculine dress code should be seen as a politically irresponsible or radical act for gay men and whether leather-clad lesbian bikers should be allowed to lead a Gay Pride parade. The one great leap forward and two shuffling steps backward dance was particularly popular in those confusing times of radical change. In the early years of the Cuban revolution, the emancipation of women was identified as a priority. Steps were taken to encourage women to participate fully in the waged labor force and legislation was passed to promote a more equal division of labor in the home. At the same time, Cubans continued to define homosexuality as a perversion and, at least initially, the state reinforced this prejudice by legally persecuting gays. Emancipation and persecution were attempted simultaneously without any sense of contradiction. Men were expected to take on traditionally female-designated work in the home, and yet were encouraged to despise the "unmanly faggot."

The Soviet Union, too, has had an uncertain attitude toward the break down of sex and gender roles. In 1983 an article appeared in *Soviet Life* entitled "Preparing Young People for Married Life":

> Equality between the sexes has long been established in Soviet society. This does not mean, however, that the distinctions between the sexes have been erased and that men and women are becoming the same. It is true that the first women to be granted equal rights with men in the twenties and thirties were inclined to interpret equality as being similar to the "strong sex." They did their best to dress plainly without any frills. They wore white blouses, dark skirts and short hair. They shunned cosmetics and perfume. They did everything they could to ensure that they were not regarded as feminine, soft or weak. Fortunately, this feminist extreme, this trend toward masculinity didn't last long.[4]

The concern that women not be the same as men is related to an uneasiness about changes in social roles deemed appropriate to men and women. In the Soviet Union, it is rarely suggested that women should no longer engage in work traditionally done by men (i.e. wage work outside the home). Women are a valuable and essential part of the work force. Rather the concern about sex and gender roles tends to be directed against men taking on functions formerly performed by women—child-rearing and housework. Women are urged not to *look* like men and men are urged not to *act* like women.

In September 1984 the Soviet newspaper, *Pravda*, ran an article on sex roles arguing for a return to more traditional relationships in the home: "The prestige and self-esteem of the man should have a priority in the family ethic. A woman must remain a woman and a man a man." The author of the Pravda piece notes with approval that in the past "there existed a strict division in the family. The honor of the man was first and foremost. Women have always felt the strong hand and friendly strength of the man." In recent years, though, "too many men have abrogated their masculine superiority over women."

The article concludes "families where the woman has voluntarily yielded leadership are the happiest," and offers an example from the life of an acquaintance of the author. The woman comes home unexpectedly and discovers her husband doing the dishes. She notices that her husband is embarrassed by the situation and tries to reach out to him... "but, the poor devil raised a wet hand and softly asked me to leave him alone. He was tired, he said. I saw that my man had changed. Even his voice sounded different." The woman sees that she is ruining her husband and decides to take action: "Take off that apron. I don't want to see you in the kitchen bent over the sink again. Be a man."[5]

It is obviously not only in societies formally and explicitly committed to far-reaching social change that alarms are being sounded over the break down of the gender divide. In the United States, where a simple sexual equality amendment (the ERA) has failed to be adopted, the radical right has effectively mobilized fears about the changing roles for, and relations between, the sexes. The so-called Moral Majority has taken on the responsibility of restoring the manhood of the nation by rebuilding its military might (the U.S. before Reagan allegedly was getting soft and as such was increasingly impotent to respond forcefully to its enemies) and of saving society from creeping decadence evidenced in widespread homosexuality.

The question of manhood even became a central concern in the 1984 Reagan/Mondale presidential campaign in the U.S. In the years just preceeding the election, opinion polls began to suggest for the first time that women as a group held widely different views from men on political issues and candidates. This so-called gender gap finally alerted male politicians to women's specific interests and political clout as women are as likely to vote as men and outnumber them.

Responding to this reality, the Democratic candidate Walter Mondale took the unprecedented step of naming a woman, Geraldine Ferraro, as his vice-presidential running mate. The excitement created by this historic act briefly boosted the popularity of the Democratic ticket. But soon after, an image problem began to plague Mr. Mondale. He simply wasn't seen as manly enough. Democratic concern about wooing women in the gender gap competition was replaced by frantic efforts to dispel the impression that a "macho gap" existed between the Democratic and Republican contenders.

The Democrat's media consultant suggested that Mr. Mondale projected a weaker male image. The head of Mondale's council of advisers to the campaign attempted to repair the damage by telling the press:

> I think Walter Mondale gets a bum rap on this male issue. The truth of the matter is that on male issues—defense and economics and things like that—Mondale is solid. Even further than that, Mondale is sort of a man's man. He likes to do the things that we associate with male—what do you call it?—macho. He's a fisherman. He likes to sit around and have a drink in the evening with his shoes off and a cigar in his mouth with friends. He's a hunter. He's interested in sports.[6]

It is not only among Presidential candidates that the need seems to exist to *prove* one's masculinity or, alternately, to demonstrate one's femininity. This suggests that despite the popular belief that sex and gender are innate and inseparable, we recognize that gender identity is far from secure. To those who have built an identity based on repeatedly proving and reasserting membership in one of two appropriate sex/gender groups, it can be extremely disturbing to be confronted with gender outlaws and sexual minorities who fundamentally reject the choice of categories.

Among the most widely criticized of the sexual minorities are transsexuals, men and women who feel an intolerable conflict between their body and sexual identity. Those transsexuals who seek surgery to bring the two in line often face a public reaction of ridicule, contempt or pity.

Yet nearly everyone attempts to reshape their anatomy to bring it more comfortably close to the sex and gender ideal. Most women shave their legs and underarms because it is not only unfeminine, it is somehow unfemale to be hairy. The moustached woman will almost certainly contemplate a change of anatomy through depilatories or electrolysis to avoid being addressed as "sir," to rid herself of the confusing sensation of stubble, to ease the mixed signals. A small-chested woman may receive breast implants to help her feel more womanly. A short man may wear elevator shoes and a small man devote himself to body building to create a more "manly" physique. All are trying to fix a conflict between social and sexual identity and anatomical reality.

While it is true that each of us grows up knowing our designated place on the gender divide, certain groups have challenged this automatic coupling of biological sex to gender. In mainstream culture, where men and women more or less conform to gender expectations, it may be overlooked that men are not born wearing ties nor women with long hair. But when the symbols and the sexes are mixed, the costuming becomes more obvious. What is simply masculine and unremarkable when worn by a heterosexual man, is butch role playing when taken on by a lesbian. A heterosexual woman dressed according to the code of femininity will probably not be seen as costumed to fit a role—but an otherwise obvious lesbian dressed in a similar fashion is described as "femme."

In this way, the subculture throws into relief the hidden assumptions of the majority culture's customary coupling of gender and sex. If men dressed in standard male attire were described as "butch" rather

than "masculine," it might demystify the look in the same way that the use of the term "macho" has served as a reminder that typically masculine behavior is neither innate nor necessary to men.

Butch style, whether worn by men or women, is a symbol of detachment. Dressing butch gives the wearer the protection of being the observer, not the object. A femme-y look, by contrast, suggests self-display, whether in a quietly demure or sexually flashy fashion. Butch is a style of understatement: "I don't need to show flesh because *I* am in a position to choose." Butch is no coy "come hither" look, but a challenge—"I see you and *maybe* I like what I see."

There is something about femme-y style that in itself produces insecurity, a sense of vulnerability and exposure. The femme invites the gaze and it takes a great deal of feminine self-confidence to risk that kind of scrutiny. One runs the risk of looking "cheap" instead of sexy, ridiculous instead of fashionable. Every woman knows from media messages and experience that you really *can* do it wrong.

While butch may be more self-protective, it can be as boring as it is safe. Serious butch style often denies color and humor. In the film, *Yentl*, Barbra Streisand manages to assume both sexes and genders in her transformation from young village girl, Yentl, to Ansel the "boy" scholar. And in the process, Streisand inadvertantly illustrates some of the limitations of both. If serious butch is boring, serious femme demands "beauty."

Yentl is a young woman with ambition, but in her traditional community, her sex is in conflict with her "masculine" interests. Yentl rightly concludes that a masculine disguise will be enough to win her acceptance as a serious male student.

As Yentl, in long dresses and flowing hair, Streisand looks acceptable but not really Hollywood Beautiful. Her face is "wrong" for that. Her famous nose is not little girl pretty, her features aren't big screen beautiful in a culture that tends to define beauty as a protestant pug nose. But when dressed as a boy she comes into her own with her individual beauty revealed rather than overshadowed by her failure to adequately match a feminine stereotype.

Yet, even during the relatively short span of the film, the male uniform becomes visually monotonous. The black suit of the scholar is an outfit entirely free of fantasy. Of course, as Ansel, Yentl must give up far more than an indulgence in style and feminine fashion; she must also hide her sexuality or risk revealing herself to be less than a real man.

At the film's end, Yentl chooses to dispense with her disguise, but her foray into the male world has left her a changed woman. She thus sets sail for America in pursuit of that hitherto elusive unity of sex, gender and sexuality. Still, the femininity and sexuality she once *chose* to deny in the "Old World" may continue to be denied her in the New. For even in her dresses, her distinctly un-Waspy features will tag her as an unfeminine outsider.

In her "biomythography," *Zami: A New Spelling of My Name,* Audre Lorde describes her experience as a Black woman in the predominantly white New York gay bars of the 1950s. Black women remained outsiders even as lesbians among lesbians:

> Being women together was not enough. We were different. Being gay girls together was not enough. We were different. Being Black together was not enough. We were different. Being Black women together was not enough. We were different. Being Black dykes together was not enough. We were different.[7]

The vulnerablity of being Black in that white world led some women to develop an intimidating butch style: tough, elegant, free-spending:

> To be Black, female, gay and out of the closet in a white environment...was considered by many Black lesbians to be simply suicidal. And if you were fool enough to do it, you'd better come on so tough that nobody messed with you. I often felt put down by their sophistication, their clothes, their manners, their cars, and their femmes...By white America's racist distortions of beauty, Black women playing "femme" had very little chance... There was constant competition among butches to have the most "gorgeous femme" on their arm. And "gorgeous" was defined by a white male world's standards.[8]

The Black butch lesbian was a woman aware of her vulnerability as a racial and sexual minority but intent on indicating that she meant to be treated with respect. Pronounced masculine appearance and behavior among male (class or race) outsiders can serve a similar function. These men may have little more than their membership in the brotherhood as evidence of authority. Men with greater access to economic and political influence have less need to parade their masculinity, wealth and social position being proof enough of their manhood. Gender symbols, attached to often complex arrangements of power and vulnerability, are thus used to suggest the proper etiquette of social interaction.

The most important function of gendered appearance is to unambiguously distinguish men from women. It is such a basic category that it is difficult to even talk about a person before establishing his or her sex. We must determine which pronoun and which set of adjectives to use.

Visually violating these categories can be so threatening to the observer's sense of personal identity and social hierarchy that the response will be abusive: "hey moustache"; "can't tell the boys from the girls"; "get a haircut faggot"; "fat boy, you've got tits!"

Those victories achieved over a strict division of gender symbols according to sex have been won at considerable cost. But the desperate courage of early gender outlaws tends to be forgotten almost as soon as the outrageous becomes the acceptable. Every spring, one or another fashion designer attempts to introduce a skirt for men. But few men—even those with otherwise radical views on sexual politics or style—dare appear in public in anything resembling a dress. Rather than this being seen as a failure of nerve, it is somehow offered as evidence of the special burdens of manhood: "Women can wear men's clothes, no problem; but a man can't wear a dress." This "proof" of the greater freedom enjoyed by women fails to acknowledge the long and difficult struggle waged by feminist dress reformers.

American and European activists in the women's rights campaigns of the mid-nineteenth century directly confronted the feminine dress code by introducing reform fashions such as the so-called "bloomer" (a modified trouser), and later the split skirt. These challenges demanded tremendous courage. Women who dared appear so clad in public were punished with verbal abuse and sometimes even physical assault.

Feminism has been built on this kind of confrontation with sex-appropriate behavior and gendered appearance. Women who experienced their imposed gender role as an ill-fitted uniform thus began to create the possibility of challenging the role rather than blaming their anatomy.

If feminists have waged a steady struggle against imposed femininity, it is not only because feminine attire is sometimes less practical and more uncomfortable than that created for men. Nor is it simply a response to the fact that women carry much of society's ornamental burden and have, therefore, rebelled against the drain on time and energy required to be presentably feminine.

The rebellion against feminine fashion has also and importantly been a statement about created differences. Through femininity, the supposed inherent differences between the sexes were to be visually demonstrated by women. Gender could then be used in much the same way as race: if women *looked* different, it proved easier to justify unequal political, economic and social treatment. Women demanding equal rights had to point out the *artifice* of gendered appearance in order to make obvious that the differences were created, not innate. They sought to show that femininity was a heavy social varnish painted onto the human form.

Men may well be less aware that gender is created since man, and hence masculinity, has always been the norm, the generic—and woman/femininity is defined by how it differs from that standard. Masculine is the unadorned face, the uncontorted form, the uncontrolled appetite, and raw emotion. The necessary artifice and self-control of femininity has helped create among women a greater awareness that our "natural" gender role is a more or less elaborate disguise.

The second wave of European and North American feminism in the 1970s again took up the relationship between gendered appearance and gender privilege. Feminists spurned artifice intended to exaggerate differences between women and men and instead promoted a fashion emphasizing comfort and function. This position was articulately restated by Susan Brownmiller in 1984 in her book *Femininity*. Brownmiller describes femininity as "a powerful esthetic that is built on a recognition of powerlessness."[9]

Femininity is a package deal for Brownmiller. Wearing a dress leads to shaved legs, to nylons, to discomfort and obsession with appearance. Her response is to reject any involvement with these gender symbols:

> Why do I persist in not wearing skirts? Because I don't like this artificial gender distinction. Because I don't want to return to the expense and aggravation of nylons. Because I will not reacquaint myself with the discomfort of feminine shoes...Because I remember resenting the enormous amount of thinking time I used to pour into superficial upkeep concerns, and because the nature of feminine dressing is superficial in essence..."[10]

Still this resistance is tinged with self-sacrifice:

> On bad days, I *mourn* my old dresses. I *miss* the graceful flow of fabric...and pretty colors. Sensible shoes announce an unfeminine sensibility...Sensible shoes *aren't fun* ...Sensible shoes *aren't sexy*...They are crisply efficient. As a matter of principle I stopped shaving my legs and underarms several years ago, but

> I have yet to accept *the unesthetic results*...I look at my legs and
> know they are *no longer attractive,* not even to me. They are
> simply legs, upright and honest, and that ought to be good
> enough, but it isn't..." [emphasis mine][11]

How did women's *liberation* end up on the side of the sensible over
the sexual, the "efficient, upright and honest" over the colorful and
fun? Though women did not create the opposition between the sexy
and the self-respecting, the sensuous and the serious, we often—even in
our rebellion—have accepted these qualities as mutually exclusive.
And indeed not without reason.

Given the reality of *imposed* femininity, each woman is faced with
the choice of accommodation and its rewards of sexual and social
approval, or rebellion and the punishing ridicule reserved for the
"asexual" and ugly. For those choosing rebellion, the world's hostile
judgement is easily internalized and constantly reinforced. All of
which is perhaps easier to see if we return to the example of men in
dresses.

Should the average man dare defy the masculine dress code by
walking down the street in a very ordinary skirt he would most likely
lose a sense of being a serious and sexually attractive man (regardless of
his sexual preference). In the face of the constant stares, giggles and
harassment, most men would experience feelings of personal shame
despite the boldness of the publically defiant visual statement. They
would also undoubtedly long for the comfortable security of conventional masculinity.

Now back to Brownmiller, and all the rest of us who, each in her
own way, has challenged the feminine dress code. Is it any wonder we
sometimes feel ourselves to be unattractive, ridiculous and generally
inadequate even while professing pride in our principled stand. Or that
we come to echo the punishing judgement of our culture demanding
we choose between principles and pleasure.

Given the terms of this polarized debate, women attempting to go
beyond the divisions risk being seen as backsliders—or worse, as
collaborators with the old, oppressive order. Similarly, the current
renaissance of showy sexuality, bright color and gendered appearance
is considered by some to be evidence of a failure of feminism:

> If women in the 80s now find they are returning to make up as a
> feminine camouflage, even as they continue to raise their
> expectations, they are saying that the competition—not with
> men, but *for* them—is so intense that the historic lure of bold,

bright color and the teasing sexuality it signifies cannot *as yet* be abandoned. [emphasis mine][12]

What a grim post-revolutionary world is envisioned. Artifice-free functional clothing is genderless and often comfortable. It is also unquestionably sensible attire for many activities. But what would functional clothing look like if our intended activity is sex? Mightn't a lacy bra or sheer stockings have erotic appeal less because they are symbols of female *powerlessness* and more because they are familiar symbols of female *sexuality?*

I stopped wearing a bra when still in my teens. It disappeared from my life along with dresses, long hair, make-up and meat. Over the years only the bra remained firmly unrehabilitated. Until recently, that is...

It was Mendicino and the open hearth fire and a forbidden woman. But mostly it was that lacy black bra. I slowly unbuttoned her blouse and there it was, unexpected and erotic. As I reached around her to undo the clasps, I entered America's collective fantasy of sexual foreplay. I'd been there before, only this time I was the one with the sweaty palms fumbling with the hooks. I still don't like the feel or the ideology of "lift and separate," but for recreational use...

If gender symbols are indeed erotic then we need to find ways to allow for gender play without reinforcing gender privilege. Pat Califia poses the problem this way:

> Why was there a social policy to have only two genders and keep them polarized? ...I have come to the conclusion that this exists because it is eroticized...The differences between men and women are seized upon, encouraged, artifically exaggerated and even lied about to create a distance and a tension...a strange territory to explore...Those of us who are working for a world without gender privilege need to ask ourselves how we want to accomplish this. Do we want a society where the similarities beween men and women are emphasized, and people are discouraged from expressing their differences? Or do we want a society of pluralistic gender, where people can mix and match the components of their sexual orientation?[13]

Clothing and role playing can enrich fantasy by allowing for distance from everyday reality. There is something impossibly earnest about the demand that we feel sexual attraction only in a non-objectified, ungendered fashion. It may in fact be impossible not to objectify an attractive stranger. Until one learns enough to fill in the blanks, the attraction can't help but be built on the image s/he chooses to project and the fantasy which the observer then creates.

One important problem with objectification is that it is in essense superficial—you can go nowhere with it except, if you are lucky and so inclined, to bed. Once real communication begins, the object becomes subject—"I am not only what you would have me be." This is something guaranteed to cause problems if one partner has the power to insist that the other not assert a self that goes beyond the fantasy.

Traditionally, men have been in a position to attempt this sort of demand of the "girl of their dreams." Nor is this danger merely a thing of the past. For this reason gender play may be more difficult in mainstream heterosexual society than, say, in lesbian subculture where the competition "not with but *for* men" is a non-issue.

Among gays, gendered appearance traditionally has been seen as an indication that the sub-culture is derivative, created out of the prejudices and preferences of dominant culture. Certainly, in the early days of the contemporary women's movement gendered appearance in gay sub-culture was condemned as evidence of internalized oppression. Old-fashioned gays were seen to be simply adapting oppressive heterosexual role patterns to single sex relationships.

It was argued that homosexuality freed of self-hate would instead produce an androgynous ideal: the Lesbian Feminist Relationship. This new kind of relationship would be without the power exchange of gender roles: no more control, no more surrender, only two sisterly equals. What a picture of strength. The only problem was, who was that strong?

With its built in butch/femme expectation, heterosexuality at least seemed to guarantee an outlet for the need to occasionally let go, to be dependent, even as it often frustrated the need among women to be sexually and personally assertive. Lesbian Feminism with its double-edged ax and Amazon imagery spoke to the need for female power against male oppression but was peculiarly silent about any power exchange between women.

de quoi tu te
DANIELA

un film de MAX PECAS
avec
RENE DARY   SANDRINE   et   CLAIR
usique de CHARLES AZNAVOUR et GEORGES GARVARE
Production CONTACT ORGANISATION P.I.P.

A woman leaning against the bar catches my eye and holds it. Her upturned collar and black leather tie suit her studied distance. She lets me wait awhile before acknowledging my appreciative attention, and then admits interest by pulling herself up to her full height. Tonight she is butch in her need to stand tall and in her apparent pleasure in my high heel shoes that give me uneasy inches on her.

On the dance floor, her movements are as understated and erotic as her clothing, but more revealing. I glimpse lace riding this woman's fullness, a woman's curves and folds hidden under the severe lines of her attire. I slowly press myself against the fading pretense of butch restraint. And then withdraw. She wants feminine, I'll give her feminine: promising but deliberately delaying her release. Now I lead this subtle dance. My painted nails flash a message that has nothing to do with passivity. Those fingers dipped in blood red lacquer can penetrate her depths.

These are symbols of control and surrender. But they are fluid; mouth and fingers, sheer underwear and leather ties, teasing out a woman's desire.

The persistence of gendered appearance among some lesbians and gay men was not an altogether predictable evolution from the androgyny of the 1960s Natural Look and the functionalism of 1970s feminist fashion. Dennis Altman, author of *The Homosexualization of America* notes;

> In the early days of the movement, both women and men saw the process of gay liberation as intimately related to the blurring of sexual and gender boundaries, a move toward androgyny...Our biggest failure was an inability to foresee the extent to which the opposite would happen and a new gay culture/identity would emerge that would build on existing male/female differences.[14]

Despite the use of existing gender symbols, a blurring of sex and gender boundaries *is* clearly occurring. If the Castro Clone* look of self-conscious masculinity, for example, seems to be the image of choice among San Francisco gay men, there is still a greater awareness that those gender symbols are assumed not inherent. Altman states, "The macho cult is in a sense a new form of drag, a parody of the social

---

* The short hair, trimmed moustache and athletic build currently popular among many gay men in the Castro district of San Francisco.

expectations of homosexuals, just as was the more traditional queen..."[15] This element of parody and self-conscious creation of a gendered image distinguishes the new esthetic. It is exactly the awareness of gender as a social construct that makes the role playing play.

The most pertinent objection to gender play, both in appearance and behavior, is that it can be seen as a call for cosmetic changes that ignore—or even hide—core issues of sexual inequality and abuse, and sexist socialization. This is a point well-taken.

Just because gender-bending is currently fashionable does not mean that the sexual revolution has triumphed. Clearly, a cultural commitment to compulsory heterosexuality and a functional gender divide remain strong throughout much of society. Indeed, even those media (such as fashion magazines, rock videos and motion pictures) which seem to celebrate gender play are far from radical in the implications they draw from it. High fashion women's magazines may enthusiastically promote the Parisian Les Garconnes style with women dressed in "tailored, tweedy and manly" clothing, but implicit in the promise is that the models thereby make themselves more attractive to men.

Similarly, most of the successful Hollywood films engaged in gender games are careful to explain cross-dressing as an instrument used to achieve some otherwise perfectly conventional sexual or professional goal. In one of the most popular of these films, *Tootsie*, Dustin Hoffman plays an unemployed male actor who finds fame, fortune and the girl of his dreams by pretending to be a woman. Stardom and love are also the rewards of cross-dressing for Julie Andrews in *Victor/Victoria* in which Victoria is a straight woman pretending to be a gay man impersonating a straight woman, And, as noted, in *Yentl*, Barbra Streisand chooses to pass herself off as a young boy to the honorable end of being allowed to study.

Even more telling, in each of these films, the heterosexuality of the apparent gender outlaw is carefully established. Indeed, the love of a member of the "opposite" sex is typically cause for throwing aside the disguise. Invariably, the lovers are relieved to see that their attractions are, after all, normal. These films allow for no ambiguity. Attraction is not to the gendered appearance of the cross-dressed lover, but rather to the "real gender" hidden beneath the disguise.

Gender bending in itself is not a sufficient challenge to the fundamental sexism of society. But trespassing gender boundaries in dress and behavior can help to shake definitions of appropriate sexual identity. A reevaluation of gender symbols and a reclamation of some aspects of both masculinity and femininity for use some of the time by all of us does not necessarily imply an acceptance of pre-feminist subservience.

At its best, gender play serves to remind us that political struggle, passion and pleasure are kindred spirits. Gender and sex increasingly do appear to be areas of fashion and style rather than biology and identity. If we can speak today of a renaissance in gendered appearance—both the leather and metal of masculinity and the flash and glitter of femininity—it hardly seems an indication of a return to the days when men were men and women girls.

A while back, I bought myself a motorcycle, a leather jacket and boots. When astride the bike a dramatic transformation came over me. To start with I could not for the life of me smile. For the first time in my nice girl, socially skilled woman's life, I felt Mean. I looked Bad. I was tough and powerful and masculine. This lasted only as long as I was dressed in my leather drag, atop my machine. And even then it faded after a few weeks.

Still, leather and metal provided access to forbidden gender symbols and behavior. Suddenly the experience of cross-dressed men became more intelligible. Wearing high heels, make-up and feminine attire (the package of femininity that feminism has traditionally warned against) can be liberating for those to whom they have been denied. Maybe this helps explain the renaissance in feminine gadgetry among feminists (both straight and lesbian). These symbols are the forbidden fruit; we dare ourselves to try them again. How could this fail to be wickedly erotic?

Perhaps the most important lesson of lesbian experience is that it is only really possible to begin to enjoy appearance, gendered and otherwise, when male privilege is no longer a concern. Femininity will continue to be problematic until the world becomes a safer and more hospitable place for women.

It's Saturday night and I'm on the prowl, decked out in my most provocative clothing. I'm on my way to the local women's bar—an island of safety in the city. But before I get there, I have to pass through the dark streets where sexually provocative means asking to be attacked.

Suddenly my gender choices for the evening make me a target. It is hard to assume a "don't fuck with me" walk in heels. It is hard to look threatening in tight, thin black pants.

Dressing to signal sexual intent is a dangerous act for a woman in a world of male violence. And while indulging in the pleasures of the feminine esthetic can be silly, sexy and fun, in a sexist world the "femme-y" woman runs the risk of being seen as no more than frivolous. It may be a joy to play with fashion and femininity after all those years of dressing like men who dress badly. But femininity is also dangerous because the world remains a dangerous place for women. It is no easy question how to carry on the struggle without wearing battle fatigues.

If gender is a loaded issue, sex is no less explosive. For a woman sex can be both an instrument to seduce male power *and* an interlude in the struggle with that power. Traditional female wisdom teaches us that a woman's face is her fortune, her sex appeal the bait, her body the promised payoff. Appearance, we learn, will either assure or deny a woman access to lust, love, acceptance, protection, social position and security. How can she then look at her body with a non-judgemental eye or see sex as a pleasurable end in itself?

Being "attractive" may indeed attract power, but a position founded on so ephemeral a quality is hardly reliable. Beauty and its less classy counterpart, sex appeal, are fragile. Accident, age, a change of fashion or fortune and they may disappear. And with them the bestowed privilege. This dependent relationship was dramatically illustrated when a young Black woman, Vanessa Williams, was crowned Miss America 1984. She was presented to the world as the symbol of how beauty and charm can elevate a woman above her caste and, in this case, race.

Not surprisingly, the Miss America contest was not the first time Ms. Williams had traded on her beauty. Some years before the pageant she had worked as a model in a photographer's studio, where she did a series of photos suggesting carefully posed lesbian sex. Once the model became Miss America, these photos found their way into the pages of the American "adult men's magazine" *Penthouse*. Ms. Williams tearfully explained to the press that she had thought the shots were meant to be art: "[The photographer] said he wanted to try a new concept of silhouettes with two models. I had no idea what he was talking about...It was not spontaneous. Everything was orchestrated by him."[16] As a friend of mine remarked on seeing the pictures "mostly I wondered about the inherent uncomfortableness of oral sex on a stool.

This may be a male theory versus female practice question."

In any case, Vanessa William's claim to naivity was no substitute for the required purity of a reigning Miss America. Six months after being crowned, Miss America was forced to resign. The hypocrisy was fantastic; first Ms. Williams was publically feted and rewarded and then humiliated and punished for using her body, her beauty and her "sex appeal" for personal gain.

No woman, crowned beauty or otherwise, is meant to feel secure in her personal authority. The beautiful are only lucky, the un-beautiful unworthy. A woman is made continually insecure about her physical appearance and simultaneously so dependent on it that she will accept what she is given and dare not demand what she really wants. "I deserve love, respect and erotic pleasure" is a claim too few of us feel allowed to make. This damaged sense of self is one of the keys to female submissiveness and is basic to the maintenance of a second sex.

Not only is lusty admiration crucial to good sex, but without it, it is difficult to develop a strong sense of self. Feeling unworthy of admiration, undeserving of the desire of another is partly a conse-quence of the Larger than Life culture promoted in film, novels, television and advertisements. These media reinforce the belief that passion, pleasure, even sunsets are only intended for a physical elite. Should we, in all our glaring imperfection, somehow manage to par-take, we still suspect that this isn't quite It. Whatever it is we are now, have now, experience now "doesn't count."

Real life and real appearance are not enough when the goal is to live in a travel poster with a beautiful person at your side and in your flesh. If only we were more stylish, if only we had more money, if only we had accomplished something more remarkable, if only we were really beautiful, then life could begin.

But as it is, we know we are too flawed to deserve it—yet. Meanwhile we wait, buying the props if we can afford them, trying to turn ourselves into closer approximations of the beautiful. We wait aware that beautiful people are not old.

Political and psychological analysis are inadequate to the task of putting an end to this feminine waiting game. Images that inspire deferred living can best be fought with opposing images of female sexual and personal authority. The point is not only to increase the diversity of images of female sexuality but to move beyond the passi-vity of the sexually *attractive*.

———

———

I imagine that the hand moving faster and faster under my covers is spurring a penis to orgasm. This male sexual image is as exciting as it is disturbing. As a child, I often fantasized elaborate sex scenes, but the object of sexual attention was always me, the body clearly female. Sex was never a coupling, never even a turn-on for the men involved. Penises simply didn't figure. Men were only the instruments of my pleasure.

It occurs to me as I touch myself, that the distance between those early fantasies and this imaginary penis has been filled with many real male lovers. The intervening years of heterosexual sex gave me occasion to admire and envy the role of the phallus. My images of taking pleasure, of being sexually center stage, of shamelessly exposing desire, became male.

I quiet my hand for a moment and urge myself to think back, to remember that a woman's sex is strong. Through clenched teeth, my face "unattractively" screwed into a sexual grimace—in a not-pretty, not-seductive, not-sensually soft, not-enticing expression—I hear myself insist, a woman's sex is strong. I am central here; this is my pleasure I am pursuing. My clitoris is throbbing, my sex is demanding. A woman's sex is strong. A woman's sex is strong; strong enough to refuse a penis, to surround one—or even to create one. A woman's sex is strong.

———

Trying to sort out sex from sexism, femininity from female oppression, erotica from insult is admittedly no easy process. But without the attempt, women are left with social convention, religious codes and political slogans laying down the Line. Sex is wrong unless it is a conjugal right. Homosexuality is a symptom of advanced capitalist decadence. Heterosexual sex is sleeping with the enemy. Pornography is the theory, rape the practice.

To go beyond these cliches and open the door to sexual exploration is to venture into dangerous territory. But the risk is worth taking because correct positions are as deadly in politics as they are in bed, doubly so when talking the politics of sex.

It may have been no fun when sex was synonymous with objectification, violation or duty but it did provide a common language for women to describe the perversion of sex by sexism. The anger released gave form to a politics of outrage and an uneasy unity of victimization. An important task of the women's movement was to transform these private problems into political campaigns. Victims thus became survivors and rage replaced shame.

If we had been angry about unequal job opportunities and differential pay packets, we were horrified by shared stories of the male violence of rape, incest, sexual harassment, wife battering. And we accutely felt the added insult of the romanticized depiction of that violence in the media, particularly in pornography.

The resulting campaigns led to large numbers of women for the first time checking out what was for sale in the corner sex shops and in the red light districts. Trespassing in this male territory was unsettling. There, surrounded by countless reproductions of the female body, women were made to feel very much like unwelcome intruders. Moreover, making the trip to "that part of town" meant danger not sexual pleasure. The badly lit streets and leering men reminded us that the night was not ours.

The threat of sexual assault chasing us through the streets, seemed to follow us inside, reproduced in the porn we were viewing. Pretty clearly this stuff was not made for us, anymore than the dark streets were. "Take Back the Night" quickly became not only the demand for safety on the streets but also the slogan of the anti-pornography campaign. The relationship between male sexual violence and erotic imagery was thus collapsed from a complex to a causal one.

Not all the images for sale were violent, no more than all men were. But there seemed little reason to defend pornography on the chance that some of it might not be offensive. This rage effectively closed off any discussion of lust and erotic imagination among women for nearly a decade. Even today it is difficult for a woman to argue in favor of explicit sexual imagery without seeming to defend pornographic insult. It is proving no easier to take back the erotic than it has been to take back the night.

How could it be otherwise? Envisioning a non-sexist female erotica is a tremendous challenge while sexual pleasure continues to be flanked by its two big brothers, sexism and sexual assault. Looking at heterosexual erotic images, I find myself silently demanding: "convince me she wants this; prove to me that she is an engaged and consenting equal." Of course, most commercial porn makes no such attempt. In fact, the "turn on" often seems to be the suggestion of male conquest of a reluctant female body. It is impossible to take on trust that whatever the sexual rituals, the fantasy depicted is built on a foundation of mutual respect between peers.

Those few erotic artists intent on creating a non-sexist hetero-

sexual erotica tend to blur the sex and emphasize the romance, where women are on softer, safer ground. The resulting images sag under the burden of establishing that while men *do* sometimes take, use and abuse women sexually, *this* man is not violating this woman. Honest.

Ironically, some of the best erotic material for heterosexual women is that produced for gay men. Gay men's calenders, for example, offer the male body as an object of lust. The explicit and suggested sex in their poses frees women to be the observer, the author of the fantasy, the hunter. Nor is the fantasy disturbed by the suggestion—so often present in heterosexual images—that his masculinity and sexuality have to be proved on uncooperative female bodies.

Eliminating women from the picture does eliminate the confusion between rape and heterosexual sex. But it isn't a solution. Women need sexual images of *women* to serve as models for the erotic self. Images that show an open-eyed not wide-eyed sexuality: the bump and grind of a Mae West whose sexual posturing is coupled with a fierce parody of femininity; or the confident sexuality of a Bette Midler who shares anxieties and frustrations (as she pats the loose skin hanging where her triceps might be) but whose message remains "I like sex and with my unstereotypical body and outrageous self, I deserve it."

Creating static visual images of women with an erotic content has proved more difficult. There is an almost humorous contrast between men's calenders (both gay and straight) and those produced for women. Instead of sex, women are offered fruits and vegetables, dignified portraits of great women writers or paintings by contemporary female artists. Until recently, even lesbian images have tended to be edifying rather than erotic. Lesbians have had to make do with labia coloring books and "cunt-shaped" dinner plates.

While straight women can turn to the pages of *Playgirl* for soft porn, the images of women presented in *Playboy* are more problematic for lesbians. The sillicon-filled, airbrushed body of the Playboy Bunny not only serves as the fantasized Other, but also as a woman with whom I identify. I find myself resenting her and fearing for her. Her sexuality offers me nothing—it is an absence waiting to be filled. Her appearance is a signal of vulnerability and helplessness. Her beauty is a carefully constructed appeal to the boy protectors out there.

Those women bring to mind the victim-heroine of popular culture whose sexuality is a life threatening condition. In movies, this sort of star is a young woman whose obvious beauty brings her to the attention of a psychopath, a force from beyond or even a crazed elevator or automobile. The victim-heroine is usually unable to effectively defend herself and, should she survive, it is often only through the manly intervention of a Hero.

In the nearly obligatory shower scene, we the audience are invited to view the goods. We watch her strip and bathe—while the psychopath hidden in the closet joins us in our voyeurism. One perfectly manicured hand slowly travels down her body, fondling her breasts and thighs. Lest she begin to enjoy this, taking pleasure in herself, out pops the murderer to put a gory end to her unintentional public display.

These images are what make it so difficult to envision a woman-identified erotica. Whenever a woman is on display, I feel my anger rising. She is in danger, her nakedness cause for alarm. And her beauty is meant as no invitation to me. Rather it is a punishing lesson to womankind on how to do it right.

The message of the Bunny Beauty is vulnerability. You need a male protector. Your beauty will secure you the protector, but it will also make you more vulnerable to the psychopath. Your body is not your own, and you display it at your own risk.

I want heroines who can deal with psychopaths and remain sexual too. Creating our own erotic images is an important step in reclaiming our bodies and our sexuality. What would such a woman-empowering porno look like? To start with it would be part and parcel of a movement identifying and opposing sexism, with *pleasure* central to its vision of liberation. It would visually acknowledge the lustiness and attraction of women of different body types—a radical challenge to existing imagery which reinforces the feeling that sex is for a physical elite. Helen Gurley Brown has commented, "*Playboy* doesn't denigrate women, only women who are not beautiful."[18] Much the same could be said of the images found in the pages of *Cosmopolitan*. New erotic images full of the diversity of female beauty could help dissolve the commmercial monopoly on sex appeal and break down the division between the supposedly sexually desirable and the undeserving.

Of course the ultimate test of any new female erotica will be whether it is in fact erotic. Does it make me see myself as more sexual? Does it help me imagine myself in previously forbidden, daring and pleasurable roles? In short, does it get my juices flowing. Erotica should bring to life the theater, creativity, and adventure of sex. Sex, like its sister, appearance, should be made more fun not more of a burden. Playing with the way we look, creating a personally or sexually provocative image has pleasures of its own. Denying ourselves those pleasures because they have been used against us in the past is understandable but hardly the final word in liberation.

Betty

*"It is enormously problematic trying to live as a
woman with male sex organs"*

Just about everyone has trouble sorting out gender and sex. For instance, you often hear that if we lived in a very free society, a male-to-female transsexual like myself, could freely express himself in a feminine fashion and that would take care of the problem. But for a transsexual, it isn't simply a question of gender but rather a desire to change sex. A man wants to become a woman—and perhaps even a masculine woman at that.

In any case, transsexual women absolutely do not want to be effeminate men. This is a point of struggle between gay men and transsexual women actually. There are three distinct groups: transvestites who are cross-dressed men but definitely feel themselves to be men, transsexuals who wish to belong to the group women, and those homosexual men who are effeminate. There are similarities but the groups are quite distinct.

There are as many variations among transsexual women as among women born as biological females. There are transsexual women who want to be the traditional housewife, and others, like myself, who feel drawn to the dyke milieu, for instance. But what is common to all of us is that we want to be recognized as members of the other social sexual class. We want to be identified by the community as belonging to the social group of women.

What feminism has helped to uncouple is biological sex (male/female) from gender (masculinity/femininity). But there is also a category of social sex—man/woman. It is ridiculous to ask "what is it to be a woman?" in a society that uses sex as such a fundamental social category. People are always divided into men and women. Visually you can determine in 95 percent of the cases if someone is a man or a woman. And in those cases where you are in doubt you can always ask. And everyone can always give an answer.

As a little boy, I didn't know anything about transsexuality, but for some reason or another, I always wore my hair kind of long. I did hear comments like "that's a boy who fucks boys." I may have been ignorant about sex, but I did understand the aggression. It was terrible.

From age ten to forty, I did some cross-dressing in absolute secrecy. I had gigantic anxieties over the whole thing. If my wife had come home and caught me, I would have preferred to be dead. Abso-

Betty

lutely insane anxiety. Once I was able to break through all that, there weren't many taboos left that held any fear for me.

I'm quite proud of my body as it is now. Of course there are little things...but then I am forty-nine years old. Sometimes I look at my face and think that I still look a little too masculine. Not that I would want to look like a sugary Barbie Doll, but I wouldn't mind looking more like, say, Liza Minelli. A little more the gamin.

If I look at myself naked in the mirror, I find myself a little too heavy. In some ways, maybe I liked my body better before the operation. Oh, I only mean, after all I have messed about with my body through surgery. After the operation, it really does take a couple of years to learn to love your body.

Before the operation, it wasn't my body *per se* that I had trouble with; it was my sex. I was quite satisfied with my male body actually. But your life becomes impossible if you try to live as a woman in a male body. Do you think that anyone enjoys letting himself be castrated? You struggle incredibly with the decision. I had had a lot of fun with my penis. But think about it; most of my lovers are lesbian women... imagine the consternation that would result if I wasn't operated on. How would I make love?

And then there are practical problems of how to dress. If I wore tight pants, everyone could see that I had a penis. If I wore short shorts I was always worried my sex organs would show. If I tried to go to the local women's bar with a prick, they'd have thrown me out as a man. The whole lesbian world spits you out if you have a male body.

And the same thing is true of heterosexual men. Say you are sitting in a bar and the man next to you is flirting with you. Well, I have always been someone who is pretty straightforward, and so, at some point, I would tell him what the story was with me. And sometimes they would still want to go home with me because they found it extra exciting. But you also always ran the risk that you would, instead, get punched in the face. It is just enormously problematic trying to live as a woman with male sex organs.

I don't mean to suggest that I think people must let themselves be operated on. In fact, I have argued in private converstaions and in published articles in favor of people taking more time to experiment with a hermaphroditic solution. But the social pressure is so intense it is hardly a choice. You can never say anything that would hold true for all transsexuals, but I think you can say that for a good half of us, it is the societal pressure that convinces us of the need to change our bodies.

If you really have a hermaphroditic body—a woman with a

penis—you have become a minority within a minority. I tried for
about a half a year, but it was too difficult. Perhaps with better therapy
I could have worked my way through that. But therapy for us is not
directed at self-acceptance. If you express any doubts about surgery,
they try to convince you that you are not really a woman. But that is
not the point; we are transsexual women.

The only thing they could do for you is to help you feel as strong
as possible in this society. And that they don't do. They find it so crazy
already that you feel like a woman with a male body. Still, maybe I
could have made it with a hermaphroditic body; for seven years now I
have thought about that every single day. It is a damned serious
decision.

It's not so much the physical pain involved in the surgery. You're
only in the hospital for ten days or so. But after you leave the hospital,
you have to get used to a very different body. For example, about two
weeks after the operation, I went to the toilet to piss and there I stood.
Oh, no, of course not. And the first time I made love with a woman
after the operation, at some point I thought, right and now my penis
slides in. Oh, no, of course not.

There are all kinds of things that I had trouble with after the
operation precisely because I wanted to put distance between myself
and my past. For instance, using a dildo was, until real recently, totally
taboo. Even lying on top when making love was hard for me. It
reminded me too much of the male role. But it is all so crazy. I mean
why shouldn't a woman be able to make use of a dildo?

The most difficult thing about the operation is that you have
trouble with orgasm afterwards. After the operation, you have no
penis and no clitoris and you haven't a clue where your sensitive spots
are. You undergo the surgery with the idea, maybe I'll never be able to
climax again. But the decision is so fundamental it far outweighs the
concern over orgasm. Trying to talk to your surgeon about orgasm
can prove to be totally impossible. I think that has a lot to do with the
concept they have of women.

It is, for instance, typical that transsexuals like myself let a vagina
be constructed in order to fuck. The whole accent in this heterosexual
society is on an entrance. If you have a hole then you are a woman. But
you could of course argue that the clitoris is more important.

If I could have seen my penis as an overgrown clitoris or as a flesh
and blood dildo, I could have lived with it. But so long as it symbolized
my manhood I wanted to get rid of it. I have heard some transsexuals
say that from their earliest childhood memories they wanted to have

their penis removed; people who say "I've always hated my male body." But in my case, it was clearly social pressure that made me choose surgery. This always leads to those difficult conversations over nature versus nuture—much as people have gone round and round about the causes of homosexuality. I simply won't give any judgement.

Whatever its origin, it is never easy to be transsexual in this culture. Your body gives one message, your sex says something else. The motor that drives your transsexuality is that insecurity. And then you let yourself be operated on and suddenly it is a little better. But the basic insecurity isn't gone. So you let yourself be remodeled a little further.

I did it too: another small correction on your ass, a little silicon in your breasts; there are even those who let a little silicon be injected into their cheeks to create a bit more of a doll face. You can really keep yourself busy with operations—a nose that could be a little straighter, hips that could be rounder and so on.

Once you have developed the taste for cosmetic surgery, you start to get the feeling you can totally remake yourself. In the beginning, surgery is scary, but it can become addictive.

When my mother heard that I was going to be operated on, she said to me "you are going to mutilate yourself!" But listen, what we do isn't mutilation. Sure something gets removed, but something beautiful is constructed in its place. I think one of the reasons why people call a sex change operation a mutilation (while no one considers a nose job or breast reduction surgery that way) is that we are talking about removing a penis, and that organ has such powerful emotional and symbolic significance in our culture.

Julia

"Then came the mastectomy and the feeling that that was it for casual sex"

As soon as I was diagnosed as having breast cancer, I quickly realized I was in the middle of a war; the pro-mastectomy people versus the lumpectomy and radiation as primary treatment people. The doctor in favor of mastectomy was convinced that a mastectomy would cure me—you don't want to play with your life do you? Of course I didn't want to play with my life, but if I could be convinced that lumpectomy and radiation was as effective, I didn't want to lose my breast either.

I finally decided to do the lesser procedure. The minor surgery was followed by a five week period of treatment, five days a week, a minute of radiation a day. I was so tired; the treatment absolutely exhausted me. It really took a lot out of me, something they had not prepared me for. And they dismissed it with a cheery, "you'll get over it. You'll feel better next week."

Or I'd walk into the center and hear "you are looking great! Absolutely wonderful! Doesn't she look gorgeous?" by the head of the radiation department doing his three minute check as he breezed in. The doctors are there to tell you you are fine, not to ask you how you are. So there I was: great and gorgeous, and a testament to their good treatment.

It turned out that I had to have a mastectomy anyway a year later because another small site was discovered in the same breast. But by then I was used to having cancer and was much better able to deal with it. Looking back, the worst time of all in this whole thing was probably the two week period of decision making when I first knew I had breast cancer. I remember one night in the very beginning laying in bed absolutely panicked. I kept replaying again and again in my head a scene of being wheeled down the passage to the operating room. My breast was going to be ripped out of my body. I was going to have a gaping wound. All I could see was this gaping, bloody wound. A vivid, horrifying image.

Once I was really confronted with the need for the mastectomy, I didn't have those images anymore. A mastectomy scar turned out to be less horrifying than I anticipated. It is an absence, not a presence. My friends have said that they too imagined something like a burn scar; a puckered mess of flesh. But all it is is a clean fold of skin, smooth like a child's chest.

My lover told me afterwards that he had been concerned that, while he would be able to accept it, he honestly wasn't sure how he would feel about me physically. Fortunately, it didn't affect him much. He just said, "well, that is you, isn't it?" I think it amazing; a lot of men have more trouble with it than that.

My overwhelming sense is of mourning. You mourn a part of your body. I never felt like a terrible victim, just a tremendous sadness. I really liked my body, I don't want to have to adjust to a new one. It's a painful process, but I think I'm getting stronger.

An indication to me that I had gotten beyond so much of the stuff about my self-image was a strong visual image I had of my body as a frame or a shell. The things that were external to that shell were things like breasts or hair, anything outside of me. Taking off one of those external things was like plucking fruit from a tree. You weren't going to harm the tree. I wasn't going to be harmed inside. I knew it was going to be hard, but that in the end it wouldn't matter.

You know, it is funny and painful, but after the operation you want to be absolutely The Best. You want to show everybody that you are strong, that you can cope, that this isn't affecting you. You hear other courageous mastectomy stories and you ask yourself "am I as good as that?"

I read somewhere about this woman who had a lot of breast cancer in her family. She had decided to have lumpectomy and radiation while her sisters decided to have mastectomies. Her sisters kind of wore their scars like medals from a battle. It was her tenth year, and she really wanted to celebrate. The ten year mark is important—the cancer hadn't returned, she had her breast. Her sense was to go out and wear a really low-cut dress. But she was celebrating with her sisters and she just couldn't. She wore a high-necked dress instead.

What people do to each other. Instead of accepting that there are a myriad of ways of reacting, we punish ourselves. What the women's movement is about is finding out what is comfortable for you. It is not about adopting another set of rigid rules. I do not want to feel any kind of pressure to be told that I should be doing it differently. I am afraid that not wearing a prosthesis is becoming another rule.

It has only been six months for me. I'm not totally comfortable with my body yet. I'm getting there, but I cannot go to work without the prosthesis. And my sense is that, even in the future, I'm not going to want to. It's not the place I want to be making a political statement about this. I don't want to stand out.

What I'm finding is that when I wear a loose blouse, nobody notices. It may come to a point where I will just choose my clothes carefully and not wear a prosthesis. But at this point, it is just part of my garb. I put on stockings and shoes, smart clothes and make-up—and a prosthesis.

I still have those times of feeling deformed, when things trip me up. I walked into the YWCA near work to check out the sports facilities recently. It was a terribly small space, filled, simply crawling with breasts. Two breasts per. All shapes and sizes. There weren't any bodies attached to faces, just breasts. There was no place to change. I had to change in the toilet.

It is not so much self-pity I feel as anger. Why should I be made to feel so shitty? Why should everyone just presume that bodies are perfect? I also have personal anger, times when I just think goddamit, why did this happen? I don't want to have to deal with this.

The mastectomy has had an effect on the way I feel about sex. Initially, I was very exhausted and didn't feel free to initiate making love because maybe my mate didn't want to. He felt uptight because maybe I didn't want to and he didn't want to push it. So we would sort of end by dancing around each other, being so sensitive. I felt very exposed if I was nude. I felt exposed even under the blankets because we were in bed which implied sex.

Some time ago, my mate and I had settled on a sort of monogamy, not out of rigid principle but because anything else was just too complicated and unsatisfactory—except when we traveled abroad for our work. Outside of the country, we both wanted to feel free to act if we chose.

Then came the mastectomy and my sense that that was it for casual sex. Feeling that men wouldn't be able to deal with it. That I wouldn't be able to deal with it. I couldn't even fantasize. I felt that if my relationship ever ended, and I wanted to get intensely involved with someone new, then of course I would deal with it. But there would always be something that One Would Have To Deal With.

About three months after the mastectomy, I was invited to an international conference. A friend with whom I had been intensely involved many years back was also invited. We had kept in touch and remained friendly over the years. I think we both always thought that we would meet up again at some point. We knew that we both traveled enough that at some point in our lives it would happen.

He called when he heard about the mastectomy and I told him I

Tanya Neiman
Photo: Patricia Pacheco

was going to the conference. So was he. Oh well, pity about that, I thought. It was just sort of the irony of it. We got together at the meeting and had a wonderful time talking.

The more alcohol I consumed, the more morbid I became. I sat there looking distraught. "What's the matter?" "Give me a cigarette and I'll tell you." And I don't even smoke anymore. Basically I just said that I had had this fantasy for a long time that someday we would get together again, some circumstance when we would both be out of the country, and here we were and my body had changed. He told me "I don't think it would make any difference to me, but I don't know. And what I do know is that it will insert a lot of tension into something that was easy."

The next night we went out again, and afterwards went back to his room for a drink. We casually began to fool around when I stopped; "wait a minute. I need to know what is going on here." So we talked some more.

When it became clear where we were heading I said "I just want to say two things in case we really do end up making love: (1) I am not removing my top, and (2) it's the right breast that's okay." He laughed, "God, you are crass." And in fact we did end up making love and I couldn't remove my top. That would have felt too exposed. But it worked, nonetheless.

We spent the next two nights together. I realized later that the fact that I had made love to him had an incredible impact on how I dealt with myself. I felt just much more comfortable about my body, because he still found me attractive. I needed that external reassurance.

Kathay

*"I know sex is complicated for most women, but it is a particular problem
for fat women"*

I never thought I was pretty when I was growing up. I was just
fat. And as a Fat Girl, I had to reject it all before I ever had it. I wasn't a
cheerleader, I didn't go steady, I didn't get married, I didn't have a
dishwasher...

Of course, it was really contradictory. I didn't really want those
things if it meant I had to be girlish. Like a lot of girls, I was really
smart. And yet you had to simp into this other silly personality when
boys were around. The popular girls, the ones you trailed after carrying their train, always acted so dumb.

The combination of hating the dumb girl role and the realization
that, as a fat girl, I was going to fail the *Seventeen* Magazine Quiz, just
sort of caused me to turn my sexuality off. I didn't flirt because I didn't
want to fail and I knew it was my destiny to fail. I wasn't going to set
myself up. But once I lost weight it seemed to me, for the first time, that
the whole thing became a question of choice.

The question then became which aspects of the feminine role did I
want to continue to reject and which did I finally want to play with?
Flirting, for instance, is real new to me. It is a calculated thing I go out
and do depending on how I look. It is only something I do when I am
thin. When I am fat, I don't expect anyone to see me as attractive or
pretty. I don't expect flirtation, I have declared myself off season. I
don't want to have sex; that goes without saying and I expect my fat to
say it for me.

But the flip side of it—being thin—meant that I became Sally Slut.
I was totally undiscriminating. It was such a new experience, I had no
sense of control over it. I was going around asking for something but
not sure what or how to get it. And I was totally stunned that I was
getting anything at all.

When I flirt now, I still feel very confused. I feel like a baby in
some respects, having missed those years of adolescent training. When
flirtation starts, I feel myself marching down to the altar. This has to do
with not knowing how to say no. If someone flirts with me, I have to
go to bed with them. I don't feel in control of the situation. I haven't
yet learned to own flirtation. It still feels like an inevitable chain of
events that end in bed. I know sex is complicated for most women, but
it is a particular problem for fat women.

I recently attended a workshop for fat women. One of the most important moments came when somebody said "yes, we as fat people are oppressed, and yes, some of our best friends have been fat but have you ever been attracted to a fat person?" And suddenly the discussion sort of ended. For me, that is the real heart of the matter. If we continue to be attracted to and model ourselves after magazine types, we are stuck with unacceptance of people who are different, ourselves very much included.

Obviously, we all want to be the object of somebody's lust. But the images held up to us—especially the erotic images—are of such a physical elite. They have been plastered in front of our face forever telling us what a sexual female looks like. And yet she is no more than a rubber doll waiting there for somebody to grab her and rip her tits off. I actually saw an ad for a rubber doll—Lovely Lisa or something—her mouth open, captioned "she is beautiful, she is willing, she is pliant and she won't talk back."

When I am thin, I like to wear all this sexy underwear—corsets, garters and stockings. I always feel slightly guilty when I wear it, but I love to put it on. I feel incredibly sexy and yet ambivalent about looking like Lovely Lisa. There is, though, a real difference for me in wearing it for women or men lovers.

I don't trust that the men are going to be able to see beyond it. My women friends know it is a joke. And at the same time, even we don't know it's a joke. *Penthouse* is always there to tell us that "these women do it all the time and look where it got them; they are attractive, desired and rich." No, it is not enough of a joke.

The other side of it is, as a fat woman you simply don't exist as a woman. When I am fat, I don't live in my body. My head is going "hey, this isn't me." It is a tape running through my head like static and it interferes. "This doesn't count because I am fat. I am not really here because I am fat. This just doesn't count..."

I hate it but I can't stop it, because the hardest part about being a fat person is that it is not just your imagination that tells you you don't count. In some ways you really don't. It is an act of courage for a fat woman to even go out in public. Every day you are told "go home, this isn't for you. the world isn't for you."

When I arrived in the domain of thinness, it suddenly felt like I had a right to exist. I was a New Woman. Professionally my life was a success. As an actress I had broken into the straight theater world. For an actress, it is crucial to be thin. There are parts for women and then there is a part for a fat woman. Besides, being in the public eye, on stage or in film, means you are spared nothing.

Joan Rivers has made a career on the ten pounds of overwight that Elizabeth Taylor carries around. Look at the total mockery Taylor is subject to. We are outraged. How dare she! She must be punished because she who was once National Velvet has "let herself go."

I was thin for about two years, living in the fast lane, drinking, doing a lot of drugs, absorbed in the life of the theater. There I was a size nine and gorgeous. I had arrived. And I felt lousy. I couldn't understand it. All my life, being thin was it. If you are thin, life is perfect. Thin people don't take out the garbage.

When I became thin, I was getting constant strokes from everybody, even my feminist friends. "Oh, you look so good. You're so thin!" After a while, it became clear that, despite my great body, I wasn't doing so well. Now people would look concerned while they said, "god, you're so thin..." Still I loved it. I was thin but I was as frantic as a moth caught under glass.

When I was 130 pounds, I still looked in the mirror and saw a fat person. I mean, I knew I looked good and I had all the clothes in the world to prove how good I thought I looked. But I did really weird stuff when I met new people. I never wanted them to know I had been fat.

If I would be in a group of people and they would start talking about somebody who was fat, I would freeze. I thought that if I was absolutely quiet, they might not turn and look at me and realize I was fat too. It only recently occurred to me that other people didn't think of me as fat otherwise they wouldn't have been talking that way in front of me. But I would just freeze like an animal sniffing a hunter.

During this period, I went out for a drink with a group of women I thought didn't know me from my earlier fat days. One of them, who I later learned was active in fat politics, turned to me and said "you used to be fat, didn't you? How does that feel now?"

Alarms went off in my head. How did she know? Who told? I wasn't passing anymore; somebody knew. Maybe I am still fat? Maybe I act fat? The first thing that came out of my mouth was "do you think I'm fat?" She, of course, said "what do you think?" She wasn't going to be my mirror.

Janice

*"With my disability I have always been even more sure than most women
of my age that I would be rejected"*

When I was a child and a teenager, I wasn't in a wheelchair. I
walked on crutches very slowly and kind of painfully, but I didn't like
to do anything that would make me stand out. At the theater or
restaurants, people were always saying "why don't you go in ahead of
the crowd?" I would sooner stand in line 'til I dropped. The weekly
school assembly was a nightmare too. I was supposed to come in after
everybody got settled. God, I hated that; hated making a spectacle of
myself.

Despite that feeling of being a spectable sometimes, my disability
didn't really make my feel ugly. I was aware, though, that the crutches
didn't help me look any more attractive. At a certain point, people were
always saying to me "you have the most beautiful face." I remember
liking that for a while. Then it occurred to me—you know what they
are saying? They are saying I've got this pretty face and from the neck
down there is nothing. So I began to challenge that, to suggest "love
me, love my whole body." It felt good to finally unburden myself of
that.

My lovers rarely tell me they love me because of the way I look.
The typical man is, I think, very hung up on physical perfection. I feel I
can't be real obvious about my attractions. If a man finds me out, I feel
embarrassed. There was an occasion when a man told me he loved me
and I sort of forgot my concerns and said "I love you, too." "Oh, I
know," he said. I almost died. I should have felt, well, that's okay that
he knows. I told him didn't I? But instead I felt terrible that I had tipped
my hand in some way I shouldn't have. Here we were telling each
other we loved each other. It should have been wonderful and yet all I
felt was exposed.

That is partly generational. But with my disability, I have always
been even more sure than most women of my age that I would be
rejected. Some of the guys I was attracted to were the same ones telling
me I had a beautiful face but...

I used to belong to a group called the Sexual Freedom League in the
1960s. It was really an excuse for middle-aged couples who were
feeling bored with being married to get together and get in some free
fucking. I went into it because my husband was interested, and I

wanted to keep something going between us. I thought that maybe this was a way to do it.

As I got into it, I found value for myself. We were involved for five or six years and then it died a natural death along with a lot of other phenomena of the 1960s. It just couldn't make it through the 1970s. I see it now as a thing I had to explore, having to do with my sexuality and my attractiveness.

These nice middle-aged women would come to these parties; they would be people's wives. I'd be one of them. And we'd all be sitting around the room, the prizes, so to speak. There would always be one statuesque blonde type, and every man in the room would want her. It didn't matter how the man looked. He could be paunchy and bald and old and rickety looking, you know, a physical wreak. But still he wanted her. And I used to sit there getting so mad. Here were these perfectly nice women, any one of whom would have been just as pleasing, but they all wanted her.

I got some rude shocks, and I also got some good acceptance. I decided that the Sexual Freedom League was a microcosm of the world. Say of a group of a hundred men, fifty were going to pass me by immediately because I am disabled or not up to their criterion of good looks. And of the other fifty, twenty-five would say, "well, I'd love to know you as a friend, but sexually you are nowhere." And then of the twenty-five that were left, there might be fifteen that would say "I'd go to bed with you because it might be kicks to do it with a disabled woman." You know, there are those kinky ones. And then there might be ten who would say "you are sexy and everything I think a woman ought to be. Let's go." And that's kind of the way life is.

It was important for me to find that out. I've often felt that disabled women who want to relate to men are at a terrible disadvantage because men do buy into the good looks syndrome. Women don't so much. I don't choose a man for his looks. A disabled man has a much better chance in this world of finding partners.

Age is another drawback for men. I am fifty-five this week. My friends can't believe I'm fifty-five so I'm beginning to think maybe I shouldn't be. I admit I do feel a little uncomfortable getting older. People hold it against you. Why do my friends act so shocked when I say I'm fifty-five? Why do they keep saying "oh no, not really." Like it was such a terrible thing to be. You pick up on that sort of thing.

Often I really hesitate to tell people my age. I have to admit that as a heterosexual, I don't like men to know how old I am. Your

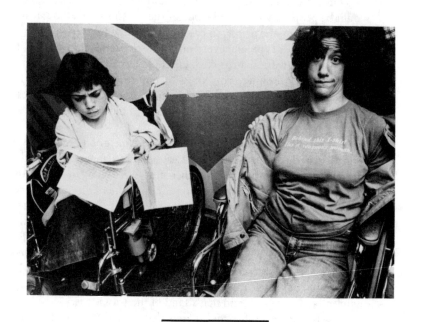

Ann and Corbett

Photo: Jane Scherr

"marketability" goes down drastically after a certain age, even in hip Berkeley. It simply would be nicer to be thought forty-five than fifty-five. A man has value just because he is a man. A woman has to constantly prove her worth by "keeping herself up."

Aurora
"The only way to keep my cultural identity seemed to be to take on that stereotype of the hot-blooded Latin woman"

I grew up in the mountains of Puerto Rico, in a very poor rural community. My mother grew up in Spanish Harlem and other parts of New York. My father is a North American Jew of Russian origins. So I have always been responding to more than one set of cultural traditions.

My mother's mother and sister do the whole traditional feminine Latin thing: lots of make-up and low-cut, sexy clothes. My mother rebelled against all of that by wearing T-shirts and pants and loose housedresses. Her bathroom has a small jar of vegetable oil and one of corn starch for powder. It is entirely utilitarian. My grandmother's bathroom is like a shrine to the cosmetics industry, with hundreds of little gilt-top bottles and jars.

Part of my mother's rebellion had to do with moving away from traditional femininity into feminism and with a rejection of the way her mother had used her sexuality. But part of it also had to do with moving outside her culture and class by marrying my father. She entered a part of U.S. society where, to pass, she had to really tone herself down. When we moved to the U.S., my mother was supposed to be a respectable faculty wife, but she talked too loud, gestured too much. Later on she began to reclaim the cultural stuff, the color and aliveness, by wearing dashikis and long, dramatic earrings. But she's never been comfortable with the rest.

I also went through a period of feeling tremendous pressure to pass. When I learned that people weren't as excited as I thought they should be that I was from Puerto Rico, I started using my nickname, Lori. For a time, I wanted desperately to look like those who did belong, the middle-class white girls. I thought maybe I could be just another suburban Jewish kid. But no matter what I did, I couldn't quite extinguish my Puerto Ricanness.

During my teens, I cultivated an exotic look by wearing bright colored dresses with low necklines, gathered up under my breasts. I think that was probably part of an attempt to hold onto Puerto Rico. I had a very sexual public image. I was part of one of the "star couples" in my group of friends and was often told that I was beautiful. But at the same time, it always felt like a performance. I felt that to be Puerto Rican meant I had to be extra sexual. The only way to keep my cultural identity seemed to be to take on that stereotype of the hot-blooded Latin woman.

But I was also my mother's daughter and was growing up during the real upsurge of feminism in the late 1960s and early 1970s. I often wore blue jeans and T-shirts or smocks. In part I chose them for comfort and in part because they were what I was expected to wear as a feminist and as the daughter of a feminist. Perhaps I also wore them because I wasn't comfortable with my body and they provided a good way to hide myself. Still, at the same time, I was really attracted to dressing up. Wearing more feminine clothing meant a real struggle with my mother and conflict with my feminist friends.

Just last year, I went out to spend some money on clothes and bought myself a lacy bra. When I told my mother about it she flipped out. It really frightened her. She felt I was doing it to get attention from men, that somehow I was selling out. She obviously had felt really betrayed by the way her own mother used her sexuality to manipulate situations. It took quite a while for me to put on that bra and not feel like a whore every time.

I recently stayed with my grandmother during a trip home to Puerto Rico. I noticed I was really looking forward to it, partly because I knew she was going to dress me up in all sorts of slinky clothes. And because I was visiting her, I had complete permission to do it.

I walk into her house and the first thing she does is to confiscate my blue jeans. She puts them away "to wash" and I never see them again until I leave. Then she brings out a whole array of negligees and wants to know which one I am going to sleep in. I just let myself enjoy it instead of getting embarrassed. In her bathroom there is perfumed soap, fifteen shampoos and ten afterbath powders. I have come to experience it as sensuality rather than a ritual you do to kowtow to men.

On the other hand, during that visit my grandmother begged me, literally begged me, to shave my legs before we went to the beach. She said she could never hold her head up again if the neighbors saw me with such hairy legs. She was actually crying by the time I gave in. It is a continual process for me of sorting out my grandmother's fear that looking a certain way is the only way to get by and my mother's outright rejection of what was stifling in that, from the sensuality that I really like. My own reclaiming of the positive parts of both my grandmother's and my mother's approaches is very complicated.

The first step in that process was a reevaluation of my wardrobe. When I came back from Puerto Rico, I took everything out of my closet that I was "supposed to have" but never wore anymore—you know, like my old lavender painter's pants. I decided I wanted to be more colorful and experimental. I only wanted to wear clothes I loved.

I certainly feel different wearing different kinds of clothing. I am very aware that the decision to wear pants and a shirt or a skirt and a blouse reflects the image I am ready to project to the world. I feel more protected in pants. But, I sometimes feel more powerful in a dress. There is a freedom of movement and a sensuality in a dress that I associate with my childhood.

I think sensuality is taken for granted in Latin culture in a way that it isn't here. Sensuality and sexuality have a different relationship in the two cultures. In Puerto Rico, it feels more possible for a woman to move sensually without it necessarily being sexual. I spend a lot of time watching the way women walk because I grew up with Latin men saying "you can always tell one of 'our' women by the way she walks down the street." I always wondered, did I make it? Or did I walk like a *gringa*? When I think of myself as a U.S. woman and imagine walking down the street like that, I imagine getting harassed a lot. When I place myself in the Puerto Rican context, it feels safer to walk slowly, swinging my hips. I don't imagine the same harassment.

The issue of fat is also dealt with differently in the two cultures. When I went back to Puerto Rico for the first time in ten years, everyone came up to me saying "you've changed. You're fatter." At first, I thought people were telling me they didn't like the way I looked, especially since I was pretty much the the same weight as I had been when I left. But finally I realized that it was meant as a compliment: "You are nice and plump." I had forgotten. For people living off the land who face starvation, thinness is a sign of failure, sickness or unhappiness. I think there is also more appreciation of women's bodies for our capacity to bear children. So things like large breasts and broad hips are also appreciated more. I spent that month with people shoving food at me all the time and I loved it. I ate with pleasure and fattened with pleasure. I've never been terribly concerned with my weight, but it was freeing to be able to eat without anybody telling me it was going to make me ugly.

Unfortunately, this point of view is changing. As people move up in class position or move from the countryside to the cities, the idea of what is acceptable and attractive changes. In wealthier circles and in the cities, attractively slim is taking over. When I was in Puerto Rico, the

daughter of a family I had grown up with was visiting home. She had
gone away to the city years before, married an engineer and had
definitely moved up on the class ladder. During her visit home, she got
into a huge fight with her cousin because she kept telling her how fat
she was: "you have got to lose weight, you look like a cow."

Skin color is another painful thing in Puerto Rico. Blondes are
very special and there is a lot of negative stuff about being dark. By
mountain standards, I am blonde. Skin color has always been a difficult
issue for me. In Puerto Rico, people even darker than I am would
be considered white. But then we come to the U.S. and suddenly you
are a "Spic."

I was Latin in Puerto Rico, nobody questioned that. But I was
definitely seen as white. And here, in the U.S., I have a self-image of
being much browner than I really look.

When I moved to California, I became very involved with Third
World women's politics—a movement that, deep down, I didn't
believe I had any right to be in. In the early days, I was often challenged
with "what are you doing here? This is for women of color only you
know..."

God that was hard. Things have changed in the last few years,
though. Women have started to realize that the ideas of what people of
color should look like come out of racist stereotypes that we have in
some way accepted.

One of my best responses to the comment "you don't look Puerto
Rican" is to say "what do you mean I don't look Puerto Rican? I am
Puerto Rican, you are looking at me, this is therefore what a Puerto
Rican looks like." It has taught me the falseness of the slots that seem
easy to other people.

Racism is a problem for people who can pass; you have to give up
your identity in order to be acceptable and you always go around
knowing that you have a "secret flaw." If someone finds out you are
Latin, they will feel fooled, cheated somehow. As if you were trying to
sneak by. Somebody who knows she's white, even though she may be
darker than I, doesn't have to carry that around with her.

There is a real mixed message from your own culture, too. Light
skinned Black women often tell me they are rejected by the Black
women's movement for looking too light. At the same time, they get
complimented by their culture for being beautiful because of their light
skin. You hear the internalized racism saying "Good. You can get out,
you can make it." But it is also saying "Get out."

I've only recently started coming to terms not only with being

Puerto Rican, but also with being mixed. I am finally starting to feel comfortable looking in the mirror and liking what I see. My hair is light because of Ukranian Jews and blonde Spaniards. I am a mixture of all these things. Instead of feeling lost between two worlds, I feel like I am part of a new people created by the mixture.

Being more comfortable with the mix I see in the mirror has helped me be more playful with my appearance in general. My clothes have gotten increasingly colorful. I shave my legs now and then just for the ritual and the sensuality of sleek skin. But my hair I have more trouble with. It has been symbolic of my mixed identity. If I dyed it darker or lighter, I would throw the balance toward one of my identities. The same if I would curl it. It is a symbol; I fought for it to be just the way it is.

After I had that argument with my mom about my bra, I had a period of a month or so where it took me over an hour to get dressed each day because everything that I took out of my closet was making some kind of statement, and what I really wanted to do was to make no statement whatsoever. I just wanted to go out there and not think about how I looked.

5
Toward a More Colorful Revolution

While feminism has helped free us from the confines of Playboy Bunny beauty, women are only just beginning to explore truly liberating, that is, playful and personally satisfying alternatives. This promises to be a project as exciting as it is difficult. Clearly the only way enhanced appearance can be a source of pleasure rather than anxiety, is if it is firmly rooted in a sense of our own value independent of it. Dressing up can only be fun when coupled with a confident knowledge that we are deserving of respect, affection, admiration and lust, even without the props and costumes.

Yet, despite nearly two decades of personal and political resolutions, most of us continue to fear that we just aren't good enough. Conventional female beauty standards have failed to wither away and, ironically, feminism may have even added a second set of standards against which we can measure ourselves and find ourselves wanting: those of the model feminist.

The model feminist haunts us with her lack of concern over being attractive. Her self-confidence gives her beauty, never the other way round. And above all, she never wishes to just "pass," to go unnoticed, to fit in. She never feels the burning desire to stop making a statement about her politics (her sexuality, her class-identification, her religion, her ethnicity) through her appearance.

What makes this Superwoman so compelling a fantasy is her ability to rise above the daily humiliations of sexism. This dream of a perfect embodiment of women's liberation rising alone out of a sea of sexism is a feminist variation on "socialism in one country"—and as difficult to realize. Somewhere along the line, we seem to have forgotten that the model feminist was a creation of our dreams. Instead, we began judging ourselves against her. To a lingering sense of feminine inadequacy, we thus added shame for our supposed failures as feminists.

171

Still we cling to this vision of the model feminist as a symbol of defiance and of the hope that individual daring might, after all, offer protection in a hostile world. Sometimes it is easier to dream of being a Superwoman than it is to admit to the slow progress made against the structures of inequality.

This dream of a Superhero is an indication of individual frustration in the face of overwhelming odds. The tremendously popular Eddie Murphy as Axel Foley in *Beverly Hills Cop* serves as just such a hero—albeit a male one. He represents a complete fantasy of personal triumph over the indignities of style, class and race. Throughout the film, he appears exclusively in jeans, sweatshirt and sneakers—and manages to make everyone else in the image-conscious world of Beverly Hills look overdressed.

Foley, Black and working class, never appears "out of place" nor fears being "put in his place." Indeed he seems unaware he should have one. He remains himself, convinced the world will come around to accepting him on those terms. And of course, in the fantasy world of motion pictures, they do. Racism and class prejudice are easily deflected by Foley's irrepressible good will and self-confidence. His no-style style is a demand to be taken seriously without the compromise of the "right" kind of clothes, the "right" language, the "right" attitude.

This kind of bold self-assurance is a heady viewing experience for anyone who has experienced real-life humiliation. Unfortunately, acting shamelessly is easier when the script cooperates. Off screen, "uppity" Blacks, like aggressive or "ugly" women, find defiance far more costly. And individual rebels may well decide that, in the long run, the price is just too high.

It takes more than self-confidence and courage to successfully resist the temptations of assimilation and accommodation. It takes support. Shelters, hotlines, assertiveness-training workshops, networking and, most basic of all, consciousness raising groups were early feminist tools for breaking the isolation of individual women fighting individual battles. Those structures of support allowed women to share both secrets and strategies and gave the women's movement a defiant vitality.

But as feminism became more an established ideology of individual equality and moved further and further from its movement origins, it sometimes seemed to be fearful of defiance rather than fueled by it. In a book appropriately titled *The Sceptical Feminist*, author Janet Radcliffe Richards, for example, expresses her concern that in defying codes of feminine appearance feminists now do more harm than good to the cause of sexual equality. According to Richards, women who intentionally fail to look "pleasing to men" have been responsible for the belief that feminists are ugly, thus alienating women who might otherwise have supported feminist goals:

> ...many other women, whose general opinions should certainly count as feminist, are reluctant to associate themselves with such unattractiveness...The image of the movement comes from the individuals in it; if large numbers of them are unattractive, the movement as a whole is bound to be so too...[1]

"Unattractiveness" is particularly inexcusable in Richards' opinion, because it is ineffective:

> ...refusing to please men cannot be a *means* to lessening women's dependence on them, because if they can afford to disregard what men think of them it means they are independent already; the most it can be is a gesture of defiance.[2]

Richards thus dismisses the possiblity that defiance might have any relationship to eventual liberation, and seems to suggest that refusing to be conventionally attractive is to cut off one's nose to spite one's face.

It is unquestionably true that the pleasing woman can use her beauty and sex as a channel to power. In film, for instance, Marilyn Monroe only ironically could be called a "dumb blonde." There was nothing dumb about the way she went about getting hers. Whether she was after sex (for which she would arrange murder in *Niagara)* or social position (for which she would marry in *Gentlemen Prefer Blondes*) she used her sexuality to serve herself. But women who are explicit about using physical beauty to wrestle power from men are particularly vulnerable to "the problem" of younger, more beautiful competition.

On the other hand, those unpleasing women who do not attempt to seduce power but directly pursue it, are pretty much sure to be punished for their unattractiveness. Radcliffe Richards' judgement notwithstanding, this is less a factor of appearance than "bad attitude."

The defiant woman's real failure is not that she isn't trying hard enough for the title of "crowned beauty" but that she seems uninterested in the competition for Miss Congeniality. Whether a woman in fact can afford to disregard what men think, once she violates those expectations, independence is a necessity. Not only men but other women may work against her, filling the safe place she side-stepped, being the good girls to her bitch ambition.

But any success acheived by the defiantly direct route enhances a woman's personal independence, gives other women avenues to power not lined by men, and frees female sexuality. When women aren't "trading sexual favors" for anything else, they have every reason to expect pleasure.

In an article addressed to "big women," but applicable to all of us in our imperfection, psychologist Jean Sarris argues that it is not in the attempt to be pleasing but in the act of defiantly resisting hostile judgement that women safeguard their self-esteem. She urges women to "give up once and for all, and with all the force, energy and anger you can muster, the role of sanctioned victim...Learn to reject insult.-..Carry youself with confidence...Insist on your own dignity."[3]

Until women, regardless of appearance, are valued as full and equal human beings each of us will continue to run up against formidable hurdles to self-respect and self-acceptance. To go beyond individual acts of defiance, we must identify and challenge the social underpinnings of our sense of inadequacy. We need to recognize, for example, that in an economically divided society, clothing and appearance are *meant* to intimidate by indicating the relative power of class position. More than 40 million Americans live in families with incomes of less than $10,000 a year. One out of every four children in the U.S. lives in a state of poverty. Nearly half of work age adult Black men in the country do not have jobs.[4] But the Reagan's have brought style back to the White House. The reality of these divisions make playing with appearance hatefully serious business.

It is hard to enjoy looking "classy" when, by so doing, one distances oneself from those who cannot afford the style, those who are still "trapped by their socioeconomic background." Just as sexism perverts the delights of sex appeal, so too will economic inequality continue to subvert the possible pleasures of style. And as long as female beauty of a particular type is rewarded by men who remain disproportionately powerful, appearance will not be a source of simple pleasure.

The beautiful woman will continue to serve as a symbol of feminine mystery to the man who desires her and of potency and success to the male who can claim her. And to the women around her, she will remain a symbol of the ideal against which they will be judged. This can only change when beauty loses its distorted power in the evaluation of a "woman's worth"; that is, when the dependent relationship between women and men has been dismantled. Thus are the politics of appearance inextricably bound up with the structures of social, political and economic inequality.

But while individual acts of defiance may not be equal to the task of defeating the structural inequalities of racism or sexism, they are in no way unimportant. Fighting the pressure to conform, attempting to hold one's own against the commercial and cultural images of the acceptable is a crucial first act of resistance. The attempt to pass and blend in actually hides us from those we most resemble. We end up robbing each other of authentic reflections of ourselves. Instead, imperfectly invisible behind a fashion of conformity, we fear to meet each others' eyes ..."what are you looking at anyway?"

We glance quickly away. Maybe this woman does it better and thereby emphasizes my own imperfections. Maybe she shares my flaws and will expose what I am vigilantly attempting to hide. If I don't look maybe she won't look. Not seeing becomes the price to be paid for not being seen, of not attracting attention. And yet, much of what we fear to expose as "freakish" and shocking is only unusual because of this created and entirely artifical uniformity.

Real diversity can only become a source of strength if we learn to acknowledge it rather than to disguise it. Only then can we recognize each other as different *and therefore exciting*, imperfect *and as such enough*.

On a farmworker solidarity march against non-union vineyards, several hundred of us walk for a solid week through central California. Covering ground at that slow, steady pace, means time to see and consider what is seen. My eyes learn to linger as one object remains in focus for a leisurely spell—very unlike the familiar visual blur through a car window.

On the evening following the final day of the march, I look slowly around the back of the van where I sit huddled with eight or ten other women. After days litterally on the road, we are dirty, weathered and silent—that rare quiet that comes from exhaustion and a week without media chatter. Not one of us has the energy to "look nice," act nice, act anything. And yet our faces speak of a self-confident female beauty, a beauty reflected back at me in each set of eyes that meet and hold mine.

In learning to look at one another with reflected pride rather than fear we make ourselves and each other visible. Only then can we be encouraged to give bold expression to our fantasies, and find the daring to do the unusual rather than falling back on the safely "appropriate."

In sharing our beauty secrets, our fears and fantasies, we act in the best tradition of feminist defiance and ensure that appearance remains a political not merely a personal concern. For playing with appearance will only be play if we succeed in dismantling the "package deal" of gender and wardrobe, identity and appearance, beauty and status.

Early feminist defiance has already done much to weaken those powerful links. The practical, functional and comfortable are beginning to assume their rightful place in a woman's closet. Blue jeans, sensible shoes and an unmasked face will survive as the enduring evidence of those important battles. But perhaps now, as our culture slowly makes room for women's needs and desires, our wardrobe can expand to include elements of style beyond those appropriate to battle dress. It will be an indication of our growing strength if accessories suitable to a feminist fashion come to include rhinestone earrings and metal studs, leather ties, silver shoes, a strapped on dildo or a lacy bra, lipstick shining sensually on a mouth framed by a downy moustache, a brightly colored skirt worn comfortably over the hairy legs of either sex. Such a move toward a more colorful revolution would serve to enhance our awareness that liberation is more than a settling of grievances and remind us that pleasure and creativity are among the goals and tools of our long term political project.

Bibo

"The movement's position on beauty was always radical, simplistic and puritanical to the core"

My family was old style New Englanders. My mother, who was really beautiful, never wore make-up. That was not uncommon. Women who were educated, had gone to Smith, "proper" women, didn't wear make-up. Women who wore make-up were working class and prostitutes. Also, if "you didn't need it, you shouldn't wear it." And the funny thing was, whenever they did wear make-up, it looked like they had gobs on because all they ever wore was bright red lipstick. Later, when make-up styles changed, women wore a lot more make-up to look as if they weren't wearing any—to look Natural.

I had a lot of fights in the women's movement because I never stopped wearing it. Besides, I had heard all this already a thousand years ago. We don't need it so we shouldn't wear it. Proper (read now to be politically correct) women don't wear make-up. I knew this argument. I thought it was a stupid issue, and in the sense that I thought it an interesting one, it was never broached as anything but a simplistic problem.

The movement's position on beauty was always radical, simplistic and puritanical to the core. People who have lived beyond that period and are still interested in those issues are all left trying to resolve them into a kind of synthesis that has yet to happen.

I had a long friendship with a woman who was at the opposite end of the fashion spectrum from me. Because we worked and got along well together, we used to have these fights right up front. She wore the most extreme example of sneakers, dungarees and flannel shirts. If she was going to see the president, that was what she wore. She used to tease me about spending time thinking about what to wear, worrying about how I looked. I would say that she worried every bit as much as I did about the way she looked.

I get dressed and there is a certain theatricality to it. But then I forget it. Because to me, it's not identity, it's theater. What she wore was always part of her identity. It was really important to her. I was into masks. I would wear a miniskirt and play She Was a Lesbian Separatist Dresser. Which was more serious?

I now have a number of women who come into the shop from the alternative scene who want me to help them make themselves over to enter the job market. They don't have any sense of what is appropriate

Annie

to pass without appearance being an issue. They don't have that bank of experience. And it is a skill.

Unless you have a whole lot of money, there is also a certain amount of talent involved in matching what you think you are inside with what you want to look like outside—and to whatever reality is playing into that, say your job. It demands skills a lot of women don't have. And a certain amount of time—without a lot of money, you can't shortcut it by buying style directly. Most important of all, it takes self-confidence.

I have outrageous self-doubts, but I have never not liked myself. I sometimes forget that there are just too many women who don't like themselves. Women who have internalized the hatred and misogyny of the culture. That is a basic and real problem: how can someone have fun doing something—dressing up—for which the basis of that pleasure—self-respect—isn't fully functioning?

Jean

"They want to get into this 'so dreadfully ugly business' but it's going to be a little difficult with me in the same room"

The most radical statement of my position would be that we are all brutally oppressed by the people who package our fears and sell them back to us. The culture is so permeated with it that it is hard to step back and see that. It isn't unique to the United States. The difference here is perhaps just that it is so institutionalized, so pervasive and so hard to get people to look at.

My world is made up of therapists who are presumably enlightened people. Yet when I try to get them to see that the most important thing in working with big people is to help them accept what they are so they can get on with their lives, the therapists will invariably answer "yeah, because if they accept themselves maybe they'd feel better and lose weight." It is hard to get clear to them that this is not the issue.

If you could ever detach it from the specific issue, like weight, you will find out that it is a totally universal experience to feel inadequate. Because there has to be something. Because women are not permitted to say "I am gorgeous." One of the things that annoys me is the woman who is well within the average weight range who complains about putting on two and a half pounds. I've actually said things to the affect of "well, I'm gorgeous—so where does that leave you?" They want to get into this so "dreadfully ugly business," but it's going to be a little hard with me in the same room.

One of the most intriguing things about the whole weight business is that, in general, it is not permissable to be shitty to people. But there are certain circumstances under which it is permissable—and overweight is one of those situations. It is understood that the person will agree with you if you are shitty to them. "Jesus, look at you, you are fat and sloppy." "Oh, I know I shouldn't be..." When someone starts into something like that and you look them in the eye and say stop now, they stop. Because that is the kind of stuff you only pull with someone who is a victim.

What horrifies, terrifies, appalls me is that women are such easy victims. Instead of saying "fuck you, I'll shove your teeth down your throat with your bullshit about weight," women go for it. Women have trouble recognizing that that kind of stuff is hostility. It is not concern, it is not a social opener, it is hostility. Because women don't know how to say "listen, you hostile bastard, I don't ever want to hear that kind of stuff again."

What is really a sad commentary on the society is that a lot of people are going around with a lot of hostile stuff looking for somebody that looks like a victim. And weight is a perfect opportunity.

I was recently out at the university swimming pool when a couple of little teenagers started up on the weight thing. I told them, "you know, I might be overweight, but you are going to be cruel and vicious for a lifetime. It's going to be a curse. I wish you the joy of it." But think about what that experience would have been for most big women. I mean, it takes so much to work oneself up to be able to appear in public in a bathing suit, and then these gals make their nasty remarks and the woman retreats in tears and for the next fifteen years never gets a suntan.

I come from a family of fairly big women, but I am probably the only one who has anything but an extremely self-deprecating view of weight. My mother is taller than I and usually quite a bit bigger than I am now. My grandmothers on both sides were big, and my great aunt was very large.

The rituals and attitudes around food when the family got together were painful. All these women who had to be persuaded to take a second helping. "Oh no, no, no. Really, oh no." They would carry on and carry on and finally do it. And then they would all sit around afterwards lightly pounding on their chests to produce a belch, mouths turned downward, disgusted and angry with themselves. "I did it wrong again." Not able to really fully enter into the holiday spirit because the ambivalence around food was so profound. On the one hand, they had cooked up great quantities of it, and it was good food. On the other hand, "but I know I shouldn't."

My maternal grandmother had a proposal in her sixties. My great aunt was involved in a menage à trois up into her fifties. So all this stuff about how awful and ugly and unappealing weight makes you, well, they did just fine. But they couldn't see it. Attractiveness has become detached from its object. If the object of attractiveness is to attract members of the opposite sex, or in some cases members of the same sex, weight is not that big a deal.

There was a lot of pressure on me to lose weight on the grounds that I would be more beautiful, more attractive. A statement of my independence became importantly "take me as I am." And I was succesful in that, in large part, because what people are looking for in other people doesn't have quite as much to do with appearance as one would think. You can depend in a social situation on the fact that everybody else is extremely nervous. If you can master your own nervousness and talk to them, you are set. Where big women are defeated in this is that they are invariably so self-deprecating that they are the most nervous people there.

I think you can't grow up in this society without some degree of ambivalence about your body if you are big. Of course, I too hear that self-critical voice but I will only listen to it up to a certain point and then I let it go. But I do feel the pressure. Going to a department store and looking in the three-way mirrors I find myself thinking "oh, Jesus.... But now that Macy's has this Big Women's Department, I can go there, and for the first time, try on clothes that are too big for me. It feels great to stand in front of the mirrors and say "oh, my, this doesn't fit at all. I've got to find something smaller."

So when I say "I'm gorgeous" it is partly a ploy and partly I really mean it. I have enough nerve to bring it off, but I certainly have my own insecurities. Yet, at some pretty profound level, I really do mean it. I am a good person, smart, hard-driving, good employee, kind sustaining, long term. What is it that could possibly cancel all that out and make somebody not want to see me as pretty hot stuff? But so badly undermined is most big women's self-confidence, that they cannot ask that question. Why is it with all this that I am supposed to be able to tap dance too?

Keetje

Keetje

"There is no reason in the world why we shouldn't take pleasure in dressing up at our age"

I am seventy-nine years old so it seems to me I don't have much choice anymore about whether I like my body. Sometimes I look around at my contemporaries and think that I am particularly wrinkled. But then my daughter says it's just that my eyesight isn't as good as it used to be so I don't see other people's wrinkles as well as I do my own. In any case, it is just one of those things I can't change so I don't worry much about it.

But getting older has always been relatively easy for me. I suppose if you were really beautiful when you were young, and had gotten used to using your appearance to get what you needed, then getting older could be quite distressing. But I was never especially beautiful, so I never had the sense that I was forced to surrender something to age.

My older sister was the pretty one with blonde hair and blue eyes and regular features. My grandmother always used to tell me it doesn't matter if you are pretty or not, so long as you are sweet. But it occurred to me early on that I wasn't very sweet either, so instead I decided to be outrageous.

I've been fashion conscious my entire life. It was always my goal to be striking because I found nothing worse than not being noticed. People could say "what a bitch" or "what a horrid outfit," but it shouldn't happen that I would have been somewhere and afterward people would say "oh, was Keetje there? I didn't notice her."

The way you dress has a tremendous impact on the way people respond to you. I think that, if anything, this only gets stronger the older you get. I have actually done some experimenting with this. I will first go into a store dressed like an old lady in little old lady clothes. Then I go into the store as an old lady (you can't do much about that part of it, can you?) but dressed in contemporary fashion.

When I was wearing the old fashioned stuff, the sales personnel were absolutely unwilling to show me anything at all stylish, even when I specifically requested that they do so. "I am afraid we have very little in your size, madame, and what we do have wouldn't be appropriate for you."

But when I came in dressed more like I am now in my hot pink sweater and skirt combination, their attitude changed completely. "I have a wonderful jacket in size forty-six, but it runs large—try it." It was a bright red jacket no less. It was not expensive and it was really nice.

A while back, I saw a pair of short white leather boots with low heels in a store window. I thought they'd be fantastic under long pants, so I went in and asked to see them. The sales clerk took them out of the window and handed them to me. But when I said I'd like to try them on, she sputtered "surely they're not for you!" "No," I replied, "they're for my grandmother, but don't worry we wear the same size."

Contemporary fashion should be available for older people. Why are we always expected to wear classic, conservative and boring styles? If I go talk to a group of seniors who really need pepping up, I wear my provocation outfit—a bright red skirt, black boots and large red hat. I do it to shake them awake. There is no reason in the world why we shouldn't take pleasure in dressing up at our age.

Sometimes minor alterations need be made in order for a piece of clothing to be suitable for the older consumer. Perhaps it needs to be made in larger sizes or slightly shorter since older people tend to shrink some. But the style doesn't have to be so different. A pair of fashionable pants can be suitable for all ages if the zipper tab is made slightly larger for some of us so we can grab on to it easier.

One major department store did develop some clothing with special features for the elderly and disabled. They created a special section of the store for them, and it remained completely empty. No one wanted to be identified as old. The store then moved the special clothing into the regular men's and women's departments and hung it right there on the racks with the other clothes. It worked like a dream.

Still, manufacturers are reluctant to create anything really fashionable for older people. Stylish clothing is directed at the young and beautiful, two concepts that clothing manufacturers can't seem to separate out. I went in to talk to the public relations man from one of the country's biggest department store chains about this. His response? "Older people aren't really interested in fashion. They find practical considerations like quality and durability more important than style."

When I told him that I had just bought a colorful green cape which was both fashionable and comfortable he responded, "yes, but you speak only for yourself. You're simply not the average older customer. If I told our buyer that a seventy-nine year old woman had bought that cape, he would burst out laughing. He simply wouldn't believe it."

It is so important to look good and feel part of contemporary society. It is absolutely ridiculous to say that older people are more interested in quality than style. I am seventy-nine years old, I'm not going to make it to a hundred. And I should worry about durability?

Annelies

Annelies

"I would sew something outrageous, wear it around the house for a month or so, and then, if I was feeling particularly strong, I'd wear it out onto the streets"

As a child, I never doubted that I was beautiful. I remember studying people on the streets, noticing the Indonesian children, and later the few Surinamese, but always hoping to see really dark children, even darker than me. I thought they were the most beautiful. And in the summer, I loved the fact that my skin color deepened and I could be seen to be unmistakeably Black. Then it was even sillier to try to pass, to behave as white as possible. When I was noticeably darker, I felt better able to define myself and claim that difference as my own.

And difference was what it was about. Not only was I Black in a predominantly white society, I was Black in a white family. Naturally I've known my whole life I was adopted which in itself was no big deal. I'm tremendously proud of both my natural and adoptive mothers, two very courageous women. My natural mother was a white Dutch woman impregnated by a man from Ghana. She had great plans for her life, and getting pregnant at that point was not among them. She walked around for nine months with a big belly and then chose to return to the life she had planned for herself. I think I have always instinctively respected that decision, though only in the past couple of years have I thought through the politics of adoption.

Adoption is one more institution that separates women into "bad women" and "good women." Mothers who leave their children are *bad* and must never be spoken of, whereas adoptive mothers are amazing Superwomen to be placed on an impossible pedestal.

The biggest problem for me growing up in my adoptive family was learning how to handle racism. White parents simply can't provide a living example for you. My parents tried to raise me as a child who could survive racism by giving me a strategy they thought suitable. Their answer was to teach me to adapt and to rise above it. At least I had the advantage of being a head taller than everyone around me.

But by age twelve or thirteen, I had figured out that survival had to do with identity and consciously started searching for what amounted to Black role models. I began reading James Baldwin, listening to soul music, studying Tina Turner's every move. I had to find a culture that looked like me. I had no Black foothold; not in the way Surinamese girls had their mothers, sisters and aunts, their home cul-

ture, their language to help them to know what it was to be a Black
woman.

I did sometimes hang out with Surinamese, but there too I was
sort of an outsider. It was confusing for everybody. People generally
assumed I too was Surinamese and would often start speaking to me in
Sranantongo. Then I would have to explain that I was not from
Surinam, but I tried not to offer any additional information about what
my background *did* happen to be. I was proud of my color but not of
my uncertain geneology. When really pushed, I gave a rather vague
answer to the effect that I had a complicated family with Dutch,
German, Jewish, Asian and African roots.

Race wasn't the only confusing part of my identity. I was female
but really couldn't identify with other little girls. In elementary
school, girls just seemed boring. They wore dresses and couldn't play
rough or they'd get them dirty. My parents were wonderful about
letting me go my own way. They even let me wear pants all the time.

But when I reached secondary school, my parents made it clear it
was time I started acting like a girl. Acting like a girl? But I was a girl.
Never had been anything else. Still now it was time I started behaving
like one. I quickly figured out what that meant when we went to buy
new school clothes for me. Apparently being a girl meant wearing
skirts. I was now supposed to start paying attention to my appearance.

That was also the period in which the girls started to compete
with each other for the boys' attention—something else that didn't
make any sense to me. And boys, who had always been good buddies,
suddenly started coming out with stuff like "hey baby, wanna do it?" I
soon discovered that being Black and a girl carried another whole set of
meanings with it, like "she must be good in bed." To be a Black female
was to be available. I remember thinking "who the hell are they talking
about? They can't mean me."

So there I was in my new skirts feeling uncomfortable as hell,
aware that I looked like something I wasn't to the boys and, in any
case, failing to look like what I *was* supposed to be as a girl. After all,
most of what was considered essential to acceptable femininity only
applied to *white* girls.

If you looked in the pages of the girls' magazines or at the pictures
in the advertisements or read the "fashion and make-up tips for
teens," the assumption was that everyone was blonde and blue eyed.
Clearly it didn't apply to me. It never applied to me. In some ways this
actually helped me escape from the pressure to conform. I couldn't.

Still, my parents continued to believe that adapting was my best bet and had their ideas of how I could be presentable.

So, for instance, I wore my hair straight and long in keeping with my parents' idea of acceptable feminine appearance. Except of course my hair is kinky curly; from age six or seven, it was ironed straight. That was awful enough, but could be endured. The really terrible part was that whenever I was outside I was constantly concerned about humidity. If my hair became damp it would immediately become frizzy again.

In the area where we lived, there just weren't any other Blacks. Maybe if there had been, my parents would have had an easier time imagining other ways for me to look. Instead they had a terribly limited idea of what was possible for their daughter.

Finally, when I was sixteen, I was allowed to go to a really expensive hairdresser, photo of Angela Davis in hand, and have my hair cut like hers. I'll never forget how it felt to sit there, looking in the mirror and feeling my head become so much lighter.

With so few real life models for myself as a Black woman, I created images from my fantasy. I drew cartoon characters, and made stories about two Black girls, Anne and Lies, who had all kinds of adventures together. I made paper dolls of them and then cut out costumes for them to wear. I drew lots of those paper dolls, all with brown skin, and wearing all the imaginable costumes I would have liked to wear.

At eighteen, when I moved away from home, I finally gave expression to those images I had of myself. I wore all kinds of clothes together; things that absolutely refused to match. I still have all the clothes from that period. I'm not sure why I hang onto them; I suppose they represented freedom.

Finally I sort of settled on a style of pants, shirt and tie, vest and sports coat and everything in earth colors. I haven't any real idea how other people reacted to the way I dressed then. I think I purposely refused to notice. Instead, I just put on an arrogant face, pulled my cap down over my eyes and didn't pay any attention to the rest.

Very gradually I began to play with things like jewelry, brighter colors and make-up. Not that I really knew how to make myself up, but I figured if I could draw I could just as well paint my own face as anything else.

Around that time I made myself some really short skirts, but I was afraid to wear them outside for fear I would encourage the stereotype of the hot Black woman who is good in bed. On the street, I preferred to be harassed because of my cap, tie and tough mannerisms than to have to listen to catcalls and whistles. It never bothered me to confuse people about my sex—"yes, sir, can I help you?" How little imagination most people have! Their ideas of male and female are so terribly narrow. The apology,"oh, sorry ma'am," felt equally ridiculous. I am no more a ma'am than a sir.

Those experiences made clear once more how everything was focused on being a girl or being a boy. And yet I kept feeling that the divisions weren't appropriate to me. When I was younger, I used to think girls annoying, but as I got older I discovered that while that was a passing phase, boys seemed to be *structurally* annoying. I had left secondary school with the hope that boys would again become good buddies, especially since I had written the girls off long ago. But by the time I hit eighteen or nineteen, it was clear that, no, the boys were permanently crazy.

About the same time, I found that there were in fact girls like myself with whom you could hang out, who liked to play chess, and who didn't talk endlessly about David Cassidy. And I also discovered there were words for the feelings I had. I had so often been so in love with women—girls in higher grades, my German teacher, really classic stuff—but I had never called it anything. And then finally it had a name—lesbian. It was such a fine feeling of recognition; that means *me*. Particularly because most things *didn't* mean me.

Another nice thing about the lesbian world was that people were into experimenting with clothes. Lots of other girls were walking around in sports coats and ties. Of course, that also meant that coats and ties quickly became impossibly boring. Seeing so many others wearing what had been *my* look of rebellion made me want to try something very different.

I started going into department stores searching for particular and unusual colors and patterns. But, if it wasn't currently fashionable, I just couldn't find it. I finally had to admit that I wasn't likely to find what I was after on the shelves and would have to make it myself. From that moment on, I became less and less willing to compromise on what I wanted.

I began transforming my drawings into patterns and the patterns into outfits, constantly daring myself to do more with color, forms and motifs. I would sew something outrageous, wear it around the house for a month or so, and then, if I was in an angry mood or feeling particularly strong, I would wear it out on to the streets for the first time.

The last things to leave my closet were the short skirts. But finally I did start wearing them—and on the streets too. Other peoples' reactions, including "Black women are good in bed," stopped mattering so much. I had finally figured out that the good girl/bad girl distinctions weren't really going to be subverted by me refusing to wear bad girl clothes.

A lot of women do their utmost to be good rather than following their own fantasies. And especially for Black women that is a never ending race, because you are never good enough. You can look really beautiful, you can even be seen as sexually attractive, but the very next moment, someone may just spit in your face. And once you figure that out, you can decide to stop trying. Then your own imagination is the only thing that's left.

I think my imagination has been my most important tool of survival; imagination and a certain amount of nerve. With a piece of cloth and a sewing machine, I can take what's in my head and make it visible and eventually I always convince myself to pull it over my ass and go out the door.

After
Word

Some of the material in this book first appeared in the pages of my journal. There I could answer back to attack as I had felt unable to do on the street. There I could recover my self-confidence by rewriting shame into anger. But over time, talking to myself felt increasingly inadequate. My private conversations still left me vulnerable to harassment; my apparent silence suggesting I would accept insult.

The decision to break that silence in the form of a book had everything to do with my job at the Transnational Institute ("TNI", the European center of the Washington-based progressive think tank, the Institute for Policy Studies). Prior to my six year stint at the TNI, Books were magic objects created by mysterious and surely marvelous beings, Writers. Working for people whose job it was to write books quickly convinced me that neither the product nor the producers were necessarily flawless. And gradually the idea began to take shape: "Maybe *I* could do that, too..."

But the distance between those who wrote books and the rest of us in the institutional community felt clearly marked. Within the ranks of the TNI/IPS, one is either a scholar or a member of the support staff. The intellectuals are overwhelmingly male, and aptly called "Fellows." I initially was hired as an administrator with the word assistant tacked on for good measure. What better way to challenge that hierarchy, to escape the function of appendage to someone else's brain, than for an assistant to write her own book?

By choosing to package my concerns between two covers, I hoped to make clear how serious I believed the issue of appearance to be. I meant to tell my colleagues, in a form familiar to them, that the preference for attractive and accommodating secretaries or the choice of young and beautiful second wives had a political dimension. Perhaps by putting it in writing I could bypass the institutional hearing problem that seemed to screen out voices too highly pitched and messages with a content too close to home.

I believed then, as I do now, that that willful deafness has to be challenged because the institute is a far too valuable resource for women to ignore. Thankfully allies within were to be found. For every dismissive comment I received ("sex is simply not a political issue," "beauty is only a white, middle class concern," "no, but seriously, where do you think the most beautiful women in the world can be found?") I was offered serious criticism and support: Mark Hertsgaard who really listened when I said "I want to write a book" and showed me how to do a book proposal; Susan George who simply said "It is important. And you can do it"; John Berger who carefully commented on everything I gave him, and who, with characteristic kindness, concluded "work well, keep well, ignore everything you think stupid"; Jan Joost Teunissen and Peter Weiss who never forgot to ask for progress reports, genuinely concerned that I succeed; Barbara Ehrenreich and Isabel Letelier who provided reality checks on sexism in and outside the TNI; John Cavanagh and Debbie Smith who helped me move the issue beyond the borders of individual experience by providing material on the global image makers, multinational corporations; and Diana de Vegh who, by never letting me do battle alone, helped me feel that my work—both on the book and within the institute—was meaningful.

Still, neither the encouragement of those institute colleagues who supported me, nor the desire to prove myself to those who did not, can explain this book. In the course of the years it took to write these pages, I engaged in hundreds of discussions, interviews and casual conversations in which my beauty secret was the opener. Gradually it lost its sting; indeed soon it felt neither shameful nor secret. That growing strength is both responsible for and due to the writing of this book, and provided the most powerful motivation for finishing it.

Particularly important to me were the women who consented to be interviewed. Sharing secrets isn't easy. And their courage helped me feel less exposed as I revealed my own. Though it has been impossible to include all of the interviews, this book reflects each of those talks. Many of my most "original" ideas were formed during those sessions.

Despite the many conversations, writing itself was unavoidably solitary work. It is all too easy to lose a sense of progress without the small but regular accomplishments of more ordinary labor. And without that daily proof of competence, without the gauge of co-workers' respect, it can be a real struggle to maintain a sense of self-confidence.

Friends—Cynthia Enloe, Kathryn Johnson, Lisa Kokin, Abbie Mitchell, John O'Brien, Janet Rodenburg, Ans Sarianamual, Aafke Steenhuis, Stephanie Urdang, Leah Warn—were essential in helping me feel connected by providing indispensible encouragement and criticism. Cynthia Saffir, best buddy and ace editor and Kathy Glimn, ace critic, were especially generous with their time and editorial skills.

This would be a *very* different book if not for the powerfully expressive photographs accompanying the text. I am grateful to the photographers and to the women photographed for bringing the subject alive. I am particularly indebted to Gon Buurman who spent months with me searching her archives for just the right images.

Those nearest to me, that family of friends who make Amsterdam home, carried me through alternate bouts of panic and procrastination, patiently listening to my fears: "This bit is way too emotional, isn't it? I'm sure the next part is too dry. The book is simply not serious enough. Do you think I am losing my sense of humor? Maybe I should start all over again. I'll never get it finished. I'll never get it published. Someone else will write it first..." Thank you to Piet Rodenburg who held me when the bullying on the streets became too much and first urged me to write this book; to Martha McDevitt and Pattie Slegers who read and discussed draft after draft of the text with me; to Mary Wings, supplier of notebooks, carrying cases and snappy one-liners, who formed the other half of an invaluable "writer's support group"; and to Liliane Maesen who made me remember my own beauty by looking at me long and lovingly.

Choosing to publish work this personal carries with it an important risk: inadvertently hurting others. My once private concerns, now made public, will surely change not only my own life but also and especially that of my family. I feel pride in my parents' personal courage and gratitude for their confidence in me.

Reading other books, I remember puzzling over those seemingly obligatory statements absolving all persons just acknowledged and thanked of responsibility for the final text. Now, my own book in hand, I understand all too well the purpose of such an escape clause. Not only do I fully accept as mine all errors in this work, I should make very clear that the responsibility for particularly outrageous and possibly objectionable opinions rests firmly with me alone. Neither the women interviewed, nor friends, nor family necessarily agree with anything found in these pages.

Finally, I want to acknowledge a tremendous debt to the women whose writing on these issues preceeded mine. Some of them are quoted extensively in this book, while others are a more silent influence. Reading their work and following the discussions each inspired, helped me make sense of my own experience, generalizing what I feared to be entirely specific. Their struggles created a place for mine, their theoretical speculations offered me a foundation on which to build. My occasional, and sometimes pointed, disagreements with their conclusions does nothing to diminish my appreciation of their work. Those differences helped me to formulate questions of my own. Now as I complete work on my book, I am aware how difficult it must have been for each of those women to put a period behind her thoughts and make them public. Because intellectual inquiry, much like living beauty, can be most fairly described in terms of constant change.

One of the most alarming things about writing a book is the idea that once it is published, everything I have written will be fixed in print. And what if I change my mind? And of course I *will* change my mind as soon as readers start pointing out the weaknesses in the argument and building on its strengths. Risking being wrong is easy compared to the alarming prospect of forever being held to these ideas in their current form. This book should be seen as one contribution to a conversation that will keep us all talking for a very long time.

Foot Notes

Changing Landscapes

1. Goodman, Ellen, "The Beauty Sales Pitch," *Boston Globe*, October 11, 1984.

2. Janos, Leo, "Jane Fonda, Finding Her Golden Pond," U.S. *Cosmopolitan*, January 1985, p. 170.

3. Greco, Stephen, "Strong Bodies Gay Ways," *The Advocate*, July 7, 1983, p. 22.

4. Spalding, Jill, "Let's Get Physical," UK *Vogue*, April 1983, p. 20.

5. Mann, Roderick, "The Other Hemingway, Star of Star," *Los Angeles Times*, November 8, 1983, Section VI, p. 1.

6. Loew Myers, Edith, "Real Life Fitness," U.S. *Vogue*, April 1983, p. 372.

7. Seligson, Tom, "Billy Jean at 40, the Challenge of her Life," *Parade Magazine*, January 8, 1984.

8. Norman, Rose, "Top Czech Runner Falls Victim to Harassment of the Unpretty," *The Globe and Mail* (Canada), City Living, August 25, 1983, p. 11.

9. Pattullo, Polly, "Self Made Woman," *The Observer*, London, December 2, 1984, p. 10.

10. Wooley, Susan and Wayne, "Feeling Fat in a Thin Society," *Glamour Magazine*, February 1984, p. 198.

11. *op. cit.*, Janos, p. 170.

12. Bruch, Hilde, *The Golden Cage, the Enigma of Anorexia Nervosa*, Vintage Books, 1979, p. 42.

13. Hamilton, Edith and Cairns (eds.), Huntington, *The Collected Dialogues of Plato*, Symposium 221a, Pantheon, New York, 1963.

14. *Ibid.*

15. Spellman, Elizabeth V., "Woman as Body: Ancient and Contemporary Views," *Feminist Studies*, Vol. 8, no. 1, Spring 1982, p. 109.

Skin Deep

1. *Advertising Age,* "Toiletries and Beauty Aids Supplement," February 28, 1983.

2. *Business Week,* December 16, 1985, p. 64.

3. Bodinetz, Tony, interview 23 November 1984, London.

4. Saatchi and Saatchi Annual Report, 1982, p. 19.

5. Cavanagh, John and Selvaggio, Kathy, "Who's Behind the Media Blitz?" *Multinational Monitor,* August 1983, p. 20-21. And Clairmonte, Frederick and Cavanagh, John, "Transnational Corporations and Services: The Final Frontier," Trade and Development: an *UNCTAD Review,* no. 5, 1985, p. 262.

6. *op. cit.,* Saatchi and Saatchi, p. 15.

7. *op. cit., Advertising Age.*

8. *Ibid.*

9. *op. cit.,* Saatchi and Saatchi, p. 10.

10. *op. cit.,* Bodinetz.

11. Gay, Jill, "Sweet Darlings in the Media," *Multinational Monitor,* August 1983, p. 20.

12. Gallagher, Margaret, *Unequal Opportunities, the case of women and the media,* UNESCO, 1981. And *op. cit.,* Gay.

13. *op. cit.,* Saatchi and Saatchi, p. 12.

14. *op. cit.,* Cavanagh and Selvaggio, p. 21.

15. Bagdikian, Ben, *The Media Monopoly,* Beacon Press, Boston, 1983, p. 12. And *op. cit.,* Gay.

16. Santa Cruz, Adriana and Erazo, Viviana, *Compropolitan: el orden transnacional y su modelo feminino,* Edition Nueva Imagen, Mexico, 1980, cited in Gallagher, p. 46. The U.S. is a relative newcomer to the Third World and is not the only Western voice selling its products and values. The colonial relationship remains important. In her UNESCO study, *Unequal Opportunities* (1981, p. 25), Margaret Gallagher notes that the magazine *Amina,* edited and produced in France, is distributed throughout francophone Africa. Its advertising, almost exclusively for beauty and fashion, directs readers to French mail order firms.

17. *op. cit.,* Bagdikian, p. 233.

18. *Ibid.,* p. 123 and p. 21.

19. Grossman, Rachel, *Southeast Asia Chronicle,* no. 66, p. 6.

20. *op cit.*, Bodinetz.

21. "Cosmetic Surgery Gains in Popularity in China," *Los Angeles Times*, December 16, 1982.

22. "U.S. Sets the Pace," *International Herald Tribune*, October 1, 1984, p. 12.

23. Sreberny-Mohammadi, Annabelle, "At the Periphery," unpublished paper, Sweden, 1978, cited in Gallagher, p. 58.

24. Obbo, Christine, *African Women: their struggle for economic independence*, Zed Press, London 1980.

25. Glazer Shuste, Ilse, *New Women of Lusaka*, Mayfield, Palo Alto, California, 1979, cited in Gallagher, p. 59.

26. Choice of the appropriate words to refer to so-called "non-white" women is problematic as political preferences differ from country to country. The expression "women of color," or, alternatively, "Third World women," is commonly used in the United States, while elsewhere (Britain and the Netherlands, for example), "Black" is the inclusive political description. I have chosen to use these expressions interchangeably throughout the text.

27. Levins Morales, Aurora, interview, February 21, 1983, Oakland, California.

28. Root, Deborah, "Exoticism and Power," unpublished paper, Al Fateh University, Tripoli, 1984.

29. Conrad, Joseph, *The Heart of Darkness*, Signet Classics, New York, 1950, p. 131.

30. *Ibid.*, p. 110.

31. *Ibid.*, p. 153.

32. *Ibid.*, p. 157.

Dress as Success

1. *International Herald Tribune*, October 20, 1984.

2. Syfers, Judy, "I Want a Wife," *The First Ms. Reader*, Klagsburn, Francine (ed.), Warner Paperbacks, New York, 1973, p. 23.

3. Molloy, John T., *The Women's Dress for Success Book*, Warner Books, New York, 1977, p. 15.

4. *Ms. Magazine*, New York, May 1984, p. 132.

5. Gurley Brown, Helen, *Having It All*, Simon and Schuster, Linden Press, New York, 1982, p. 10.

6. *Ibid.*, p. 43-44.

7. *Ibid.*, p. 50.

8. *Ibid.*, p. 96.

9. *Ibid.*, p. 100.

10. *op. cit.*, Molloy, p. 15.

11. *Ibid.*, p. 26.

12. *Ibid.*, p. 27.

13. *Ibid.*, p. 32.

14. *Ibid.*, p. 22.

15. *Ibid.*, pp. 30, 68, 70, 77, 10.

16. *Ibid.*, pp. 52-53.

17. *Pace*, June 1980.

18. Brownmiller, Susan, *Femininity*, Simon and Schuster, Linden Press, 1984, p. 101.

19. *op. cit.*, Molloy, p. 66.

20. *Advertising Age*, "Toiletries and Beauty Aids Supplement," February 28, 1983.

21. *Ibid.*

22. *Business Week*, "Still Trying to Regain a Healthy Glow," January 9, 1984.

23. *Advertising Age*, February 28, 1983.

24. *Advertising Age*, June 21, 1971.

25. Conry, Tom and others, "Cashing in on Cosmetics," *Environmental Action*, December 1979, p. 9.

26. *Advertising Age*, February 28, 1983.

27. *Ibid.*

28. *op. cit.*, Conry, p. 8.

29. Chemical Marketing Reporter, June 20, 1983.

30. *Advertising Age*, February 28, 1983.

31. *op. cit.*, Conry, p. 9.

32. Adams, Richard, *The Girl in the Swing*, Signet, New York, 1980, pp. 67 and 72.

33. Krantz, Judith, *Scruples*, Futura Books, London, 1978, p. 36, 50, 62, 90.

34. In "Beauty as Status," (Murray Webster and James Driskell, *American Journal of Sociology*, vol. 89, no. 1, July 1983), the authors note: "The most general conclusion from research is that the world must be a more pleasant and statisfying place for attractive people because they possess almost all types of social advantages that can be measured."

35. Revlon representative at the 1980 London beauty fair, "Face the 80s."

36. The Tarantola Brothers at the 35th Annual West Coast Spring and Beauty Show in San Francisco, 1982.

Ugly as Sin

1. Ehrenreich, Barbara, *Hearts of Men*, Doubleday, New York, 1985, p. 24.

2. *Ibid.*, p. 50.

3. Ovesey, Lionel, *Homosexuality and Pseudohomosexuality*, New York, Science House, 1969, pp. 24-25, cited in Ehrenreich, p. 50.

4. Baskina, Ada, "Preparing Young People for Married Life," *Soviet Life*, February 1983, p. 62.

5. "Pravada moet niets hebben van mannen achter het fornuis," UPI/ANP, September 2, 1984.

6. Dowd, Maureen, "Reagan's John Wayne Image Creating Macho Gap in Race with Mondale," *International Herald Tribune*, September 18, 1984.

7. Lorde, Audre, *Zami, A New Spelling of my Name*, Crossing Press, Trumansburg, New York, 1982, p. 226.

8. *Ibid.*, p. 224.

9. Brownmiller, Susan, *Femininity*, Simon and Schuster, Linden Press, 1984, p. 19.

10. *Ibid.*, p. 81.

11. *Ibid.*, pp. 81, 156, 186.

12. *Ibid.*, p. 80.

13. Califia, Pat, "Playing with Roles and Reversals: Gender Bending," *The Advocate*, September 1983, p. 24.

14. Altman, Dennis, *The Homosexualization of America*, Beacon Press, Boston, 1982, p. 211.

15. *Ibid.*, p. 176.

16. Fein, Esther, "Miss America Denies Giving Consent to Run Nude Photos," *New York Times,* July 22, 1984, p. A 16.

17. Gurley Brown, Helen, *Having It All,* Simon and Schuster, Linden Press, New York, 1977, p. 151.

Toward a More Colorful Revolution

1. Radcliffe Richards, Janet, *The Sceptical Feminist,* Penguin, London, 1982, p. 339.

2. *Ibid.,* pp. 229-230.

3. Sarris, Jean A., "Insults: How to Avoid Being a Victim," *Big Beautiful Woman,* June 1981, p. 35.

4. Kaiser, Robert, "The Invisible 40 Million: America's Poor," *International Herald Tribune*, November 13, 1984.

Bibliography

General

Baker, Nancy C. *The Beauty Trap: Exploring Woman's Greatest Obsession.* New York: Franklin Watts, 1984.

Banner, Lois W. *American Beauty.* New York: Alfred Knopf, 1983.

Berger, John. *Ways of Seeing.* Middlesex: Penguin, 1972.

Fraser, Kennedy. *The Fashionable Mind: Reflections on Fashion 1970-1981.* New York: Alfred Knopf, 1981.

Freedman, Rita. *Beauty Bound*, Lexington, Mass: Lexington Books, 1986.

Goffman, Erving. *Stigma: Notes on the Management of Spoiled Identity.* Middlesex: Penguin, 1968.

Richards, Janet Radcliffe. *The Sceptical Feminist: A Philosophical Enquiry.* Middlesex: Penguin, 1982.

Tolmach-Lakoff, Robin, and Scherr, Raquel. *Face Value: The Politics of Beauty.* London: Routledge & Kegan Paul, 1984.

Walters, Margaret. *The Nude Male.* Middlesex: Penguin, 1979.

Wilson, Elizabeth. *Adorned in Dreams, Fashion and Modernity*, London: Virago Press, 1985.

Age

Hemmings, Susan. *A Wealth of Experience: The Lives of Older Women*, London: Pandora Press, 1986.

MacDonald, Barbara, and Rich, Cynthia. *Look Me in the Eye, Old Woman: Aging and Ageism.* San Francisco: Spinsters Ink, 1984.

Painter, Charlotte and Valois Pamela (photography). *Gifts of Age, Portraits and Essays of 32 Remarkable Women*, Chronicle Books.

Retz, Rosetta. *Menopause, A Positive Approach*, Chilton: Radnor Press, 1977.

Body Size

Bruch, Hilde. *The Golden Cage: The Enigma of Anorexia Nervosa*. New York: Vintage Books, 1979.

Chernin, Kim. *The Obsession: Reflections on the Tyranny of Slenderness*. New York: Harper and Row, 1981.

Millman, Marcia. *Such a Pretty Face: Being Fat in America*. New York: Berkley Books, 1981.

Orbach, Susie. *Fat Is a Feminist Issue*. Middlesex: Hamlyn Paperbacks, 1979.

Schoenfielder, Lisa, and Wisser, Barb. *Shadow on a Tightrope: Writing by Women on Fat Oppression*. Iowa City: Aunt Lute Book Company, 1983.

Dana, Mira and Lawrence Marilyn. "Bulimia, an information sheet for self-help groups," Women's Therapy Center, London: Women's Therapy Center, 6 Manor Gardens.

(groups and services)

NAAFA, National Association to Aid Fat Americans, P.O. Box 43, Bellerose, New York.

Spare Tyre (cabaret), 100 Fortress Rd., London NM5 2HJ, England— tapes: "Second Helpings" (1984) and "Eat it if you want to" (1982).

Disability

Camplin, Jo, ed. *Images of Ourselves: Women With Disabilities Talking*. London: Routledge & Kegan Paul, 1981.

Carrillo, Ann Cupolo; Corbett, Katherine; and Lewis, Victoria, eds. *No More Stares*. Berkeley: Disability Rights Education and Defense Fund, 1982.

Stern, Nanci; Connors, Debra; and Browne, Susan, eds. *With the Power of Each Breath: A Disabled Women's Anthology*. Pittsburgh: Cleis Press, 1985.

Dress for Success

Brown, Helen Gurley. *Having It All: Love, Success, Money, Even If*

You're Starting With Nothing. New York: Simon and Schuster, 1982.

Molloy, John T. *The Woman's Dress for Success Book.* New York: Warner Books, 1978.

Gender and Sex

Altman, Dennis. *The Homosexualization of America.* Boston: Beacon Press, 1982.

Brownmiller, Susan. *Femininity.* New York: Simon and Schuster, 1984.

Daniell, Rosemary. *Fatal Flowers: On Sin, Sex, and Suicide in the Deep South.* New York: Avon Books, 1980.

Ehrenreich, Barbara. *The Hearts of Men: American Dreams and the Flight from Commitment.* Garden City: Anchor Press, Doubleday, 1983.

Feinbloom, Deborah Heller. *Transvestites and Transsexuals.* New York: Delta Books, 1977.

Goffman, Erving. *Gender Advertisements,* New York: Harper and Row, 1976.

Kirk, Kris, and Heath, Ed. *Men in Frocks.* London: Gay Men's Press, 1985.

Mastectomy

Lorde, Audre. *The Cancer Journals.* New York: Spinsters Ink, 1980.

Media

Bagdikian, Ben H. *The Media Monopoly.* Boston: Beacon Press, 1983.

———*Abuse of Women in the Media.* Penang: Consumers' Association of Penang, Malaysia, 1983.

Gallagher, Margaret. *Unequal Opportunities: The Case of Women in the Media.* Paris: UNESCO, 1981.

Santa Cruz, Adriana, and Erazo, Viviana. *Compropolitan: el orden transnacional y su modelo feminino.* Mexico City: Editorial Nueva Imagen, 1980.

Racism

EL Saadawi, Nawal. *The Hidden Face of Eve: Women in the Arab World.* London: Zed Press, 1980.

Feminist Review #17. "Many Voices, One Chant," Black Feminist Perspectives, London, Autumn 1984.

hooks, bell. *Ain't I A Woman: Black Women and Feminism.* Boston: South End Press, 1981.

————*Feminist Theory from margin to center.* Boston: South End Press, 1984.

Joseph, Gloria, and Lewis, Jill. *Common Differences: Conflicts in Black and White Feminist Perspectives.* Boston: South End Press, 1986.

Lorde, Audre. *Zami: A New Spelling of My Name.* Trumansburg, New York: Crossing Press, 1982.

Moraga, Cherrie, and Anzaldua, Gloria, eds. *This Bridge Called My Back: Writings of Radical Women of Color.* New York: Kitchen Table Press, 1981.

Sexuality

Barbach, Lonnie, ed. *Pleasures: Women Write Erotica.* New York: Doubleday, 1984.

Califia, Pat. *Sapphistry.* Tallahassee, Florida: Naiad Press, 1983.

Coward, Rosalind. *Female Desire: Women's Sexuality Today.* London: Paladin Books, 1984.

Loulan, JoAnn. *Lesbian Sex.* San Francisco: Spinsters Ink. 1985.

Snitow, Ann; Stansell, Christine; and Thompson, Sharon, eds. *Powers of Desire: The Politics of Sexuality.* New York: Monthly Review Press, 1983.

Vance, Carol, ed. *Pleasure and Danger: Exploring Female Sexuality.* New York: Routledge & Kegan Paul, 1984.

(magazines)

Bad Attitude: A Lesbian Sex Magazine. Box 69, *Gay Community News*, 167 Tremont St., 5th floor, Boston, MA 02111 (editors: Amy Hoffman and Cindy Patton).

Eidos: Erotica for Women. Brush Hill Press, Box 96, Boston, MA 02137 (editor: Brenda Tatelbaum).

On Our Backs: Entertainment for the Adventurous Lesbian. Box 421916, San Francisco, CA 94142 (editor: Susi Bright).

The Power Exchange: A Newsletter for Women on the Sexual Fringe. Box 527, Richmond Hill, New York 11418 (editor: Pat Califia).

Yellow Silk: Journal of the Erotic Arts. Box 6374, Albany, California 94706 (editor: Lily Pond).

(group)

The Feminist Anti-Censorship Task Force (FACT). Box 135, 660 Amsterdam Ave., New York, New York 10025

Index

About South End Press

South End Press is a nonprofit, collectively run book publisher with over 200 titles in print. Since our founding in 1977, we have tried to meet the needs of readers who are exploring, or are already committed to, the politics of radical social change. Our goal is to publish books that encourage critical thinking and constructive action on the key political, cultural, social, economic, and ecological issues shaping life in the United States and in the world. In this way, we hope to give expression to a wide diversity of democratic social movements and to provide an alternative to the products of corporate publishing.

Through the Institute for Social and Cultural Change, South End Press works with other political media projects—*Z Magazine*; Speakout, a speakers' bureau; Alternative Radio; and the Publishers Support Project—to expand access to information and critical analysis. If you would like a free catalog of South End Press books, please write to us at: South End Press, 7 Brookline St., #1, Cambridge, MA 02139. Visit our website at http://www.lbbs.org.

Related Titles from South End Press

Sisters of the Yam
Black Women and Self-Recovery
by bell hooks
$14.00 paper; $30.00 cloth

Black Looks
Race and Representations
by bell hooks
$14.00 paper; $30.00 cloth

The Last Generation
Poetry and Prose
by Cherríe Moraga
$14.00 paper; $30.00 cloth

Loving in the War Years
lo que nunca pasó por sus labios
by Cherríe Moraga
$14.00 paper; $30.00 cloth

Dragon Ladies
Asian American Feminists Breathe Fire
Edited by Sonia Shah
$17.00 paper; $40.00 cloth

The Queer Question
Essays on Desire and Democracy
by Scott Tucker
$17.00 paper; $40.00 cloth

Queerly Classed
Gay Men and Lesbians Write about Class
Edited by Susan Raffo
$17.00 paper; $40.00 cloth

Media-tions
Forays into the Culture and Gender Wars
by Elaine Rapping
$15.00 paper; $30.00 cloth

Culture Clash
The Making of Gay Sensibility
by Michael Bronski
$12.00 paper; $30.00 cloth

Memoir of a Race Traitor
by Mab Segrest
$15.00 paper; $30.00 cloth

Glass Ceilings and Bottomless Pits
Women's Work, Women's Poverty
by Randy Albelda and Chris Tilly
$18.00 paper; $40.00 cloth

Shock of Arrival
Reflections on Postcolonial Experience
by Meena Alexander
$15.00 paper; $40.00 cloth

Thinking Class
Sketches from a Cultural Worker
by Joanna Kadi
$14.00 paper; $40.00 cloth

Walking to The Edge
Essays of Resistance
by Margaret Randall
$12.00 paper; $25.00 cloth

Women, AIDS and Activism
by the ACT UP/NY Women and AIDS Book Group
$9.00 paper; $25.00 cloth
Also available in Spanish as *La Mujer, el SIDA y el Activismo*
$10.00 paper; $30.00 cloth

**When ordering, please include $3.50 for postage and handling for the first book and
50 cents for each additional book. To order by credit card, call 1-800-533-8478.**